The U.S. Coast Guard

The U.S. Coast Guard

Rebecca Stefoff

CHELSEA HOUSE PUBLISHERS

On the cover: Coast Guard officials extinguish a toxic chemical fire off the New Jersey coast.
Frontispiece: A photograph of the Revenue Marine cutter *Eagle*.

Chelsea House Publishers
Editor-in-Chief: Nancy Toff
Executive Editor: Remmel T. Nunn
Managing Editor: Karyn Gullen Browne
Copy Chief: Juliann Barbato
Picture Editor: Adrian G. Allen
Art Director: Maria Epes
Manufacturing Manager: Gerald Levine

Know Your Government
Senior Editor: Kathy Kuhtz

Staff for THE U.S. COAST GUARD
Assistant Editor: Gillian Bucky
Copy Editor: Brian Sookram
Deputy Copy Chief: Ellen Scordato
Editorial Assistant: Elizabeth Nix
Picture Coordinator: Michèle Brisson
Picture Research: Dixon & Turner Research Associates, Inc.
Assistant Art Director: Laurie Jewell
Senior Designer: Noreen M. Lamb
Production Coordinator: Joseph Romano

First Printing

1 3 5 7 9 8 6 4 2

Library of Congress Cataloging-in-Publication Data
Stefoff, Rebecca, 1951-
The U.S. Coast Guard/Rebecca Stefoff.
p.   cm.—(Know your government)
Bibliography: p.
Includes index.
Summary: Surveys the history of the Coast Guard, describing its structure, current function, and
influence on American society.
ISBN 1-55546-126-3
      0-7910-0908-4 (pbk.)
1. United States. Coast Guard—Juvenile literature.   [1. United States. Coast Guard.] I. Ti-
tle.   II. Series: Know your government (New York, N.Y.)
VG53.S74 1989
                                                              88-29534
                                                              CIP
359.9′7′0973—dc19   AC

CONTENTS

KNOW YOUR GOVERNMENT

CHELSEA HOUSE PUBLISHERS

INTRODUCTION

Government: Crises of Confidence

Arthur M. Schlesinger, jr.

From the start, Americans have regarded their government with a mixture of reliance and mistrust. The men who founded the republic did not doubt the indispensability of government. "If men were angels," observed the 51st Federalist Paper, "no government would be necessary." But men are not angels. Because human beings are subject to wicked as well as to noble impulses, government was deemed essential to assure freedom and order.

At the same time, the American revolutionaries knew that government could also become a source of injury and oppression. The men who gathered in Philadelphia in 1787 to write the Constitution therefore had two purposes in mind. They wanted to establish a strong central authority and to limit that central authority's capacity to abuse its power.

To prevent the abuse of power, the Founding Fathers wrote two basic principles into the new Constitution. The principle of federalism divided power between the state governments and the central authority. The principle of the separation of powers subdivided the central authority itself into three branches—the executive, the legislative, and the judiciary—so that "each may be a check on the other." The *Know Your Government* series focuses on the major executive departments and agencies in these branches of the federal government.

The Constitution did not plan the executive branch in any detail. After vesting the executive power in the president, it assumed the existence of "executive departments" without specifying what these departments should be. Congress began defining their functions in 1789 by creating the Departments of State, Treasury, and War. The secretaries in charge of these departments made up President Washington's first cabinet. Congress also provided for a legal officer, and President Washington soon invited the attorney general, as he was called, to attend cabinet meetings. As need required, Congress created more executive departments.

Setting up the cabinet was only the first step in organizing the American state. With almost no guidance from the Constitution, President Washington, seconded by Alexander Hamilton, his brilliant secretary of the treasury, equipped the infant republic with a working administrative structure. The Federalists believed in both executive energy and executive accountability and set high standards for public appointments. The Jeffersonian opposition had less faith in strong government and preferred local government to the central authority. But when Jefferson himself became president in 1801, although he set out to change the direction of policy, he found no reason to alter the framework the Federalists had erected.

By 1801 there were about 3,000 federal civilian employees in a nation of a little more than 5 million people. Growth in territory and population steadily enlarged national responsibilities. Thirty years later, when Jackson was president, there were more than 11,000 government workers in a nation of 13 million. The federal establishment was increasing at a faster rate than the population.

Jackson's presidency brought significant changes in the federal service. He believed that the executive branch contained too many officials who saw their jobs as "species of property" and as "a means of promoting individual interest." Against the idea of a permanent service based on life tenure, Jackson argued for the periodic redistribution of federal offices, contending that this was the democratic way and that official duties could be made "so plain and simple that men of intelligence may readily qualify themselves for their performance." He called this policy rotation-in-office. His opponents called it the spoils system.

In fact, partisan legend exaggerated the extent of Jackson's removals. More than 80 percent of federal officeholders retained their jobs. Jackson discharged no larger a proportion of government workers than Jefferson had done a generation earlier. But the rise in these years of mass political parties gave federal patronage new importance as a means of building the party and of rewarding activists. Jackson's successors were less restrained in the distribu-

8

tion of spoils. As the federal establishment grew—to nearly 40,000 by 1861—the politicization of the public service excited increasing concern.

After the Civil War the spoils system became a major political issue. High-minded men condemned it as the root of all political evil. The spoilsmen, said the British commentator James Bryce, "have distorted and depraved the mechanism of politics." Patronage, by giving jobs to unqualified, incompetent, and dishonest persons, lowered the standards of public service and nourished corrupt political machines. Office-seekers pursued presidents and cabinet secretaries without mercy. "Patronage," said Ulysses S. Grant after his presidency, "is the bane of the presidential office." "Every time I appoint someone to office," said another political leader, "I make a hundred enemies and one ingrate." George William Curtis, the president of the National Civil Service Reform League, summed up the indictment. He said,

> The theory which perverts public trusts into party spoils, making public
> employment dependent upon personal favor and not on proved merit,
> necessarily ruins the self-respect of public employees, destroys the
> function of party in a republic, prostitutes elections into a desperate
> strife for personal profit, and degrades the national character by lower-
> ing the moral tone and standard of the country.

The object of civil service reform was to promote efficiency and honesty in the public service and to bring about the ethical regeneration of public life. Over bitter opposition from politicians, the reformers in 1883 passed the Pendleton Act, establishing a bipartisan Civil Service Commission, competitive examinations, and appointment on merit. The Pendleton Act also gave the president authority to extend by executive order the number of "classified" jobs—that is, jobs subject to the merit system. The act applied initially only to about 14,000 of the more than 100,000 federal positions. But by the end of the 19th century 40 percent of federal jobs had moved into the classified category.

Civil service reform was in part a response to the growing complexity of American life. As society grew more organized and problems more technical, official duties were no longer so plain and simple that any person of intelligence could perform them. In public service, as in other areas, the all-round man was yielding ground to the expert, the amateur to the professional. The excesses of the spoils system thus provoked the counter-ideal of scientific public administration, separate from politics and, as far as possible, insulated against it.

The cult of the expert, however, had its own excesses. The idea that administration could be divorced from policy was an illusion. And in the realm of policy, the expert, however much segregated from partisan politics, can never attain perfect objectivity. He remains the prisoner of his own set of values. It is these values rather than technical expertise that determine fundamental judgments of public policy. To turn over such judgments to experts, moreover, would be to abandon democracy itself; for in a democracy final decisions must be made by the people and their elected representatives. "The business of the expert," the British political scientist Harold Laski rightly said, "is to be on tap and not on top."

Politics, however, were deeply ingrained in American folkways. This meant intermittent tension between the presidential government, elected every four years by the people, and the permanent government, which saw presidents come and go while it went on forever. Sometimes the permanent government knew better than its political masters; sometimes it opposed or sabotaged valuable new initiatives. In the end a strong president with effective cabinet secretaries could make the permanent government responsive to presidential purpose, but it was often an exasperating struggle.

The struggle within the executive branch was less important, however, than the growing impatience with bureaucracy in society as a whole. The 20th century saw a considerable expansion of the federal establishment. The Great Depression and the New Deal led the national government to take on a variety of new responsibilities. The New Deal extended the federal regulatory apparatus. By 1940, in a nation of 130 million people, the number of federal workers for the first time passed the 1 million mark. The Second World War brought federal civilian employment to 3.8 million in 1945. With peace, the federal establishment declined to around 2 million by 1950. Then growth resumed, reaching 2.8 million by the 1980s.

The New Deal years saw rising criticism of "big government" and "bureaucracy." Businessmen resented federal regulation. Conservatives worried about the impact of paternalistic government on individual self-reliance, on community responsibility, and on economic and personal freedom. The nation in effect renewed the old debate between Hamilton and Jefferson in the early republic, although with an ironic exchange of positions. For the Hamiltonian constituency, the "rich and well-born," once the advocate of affirmative government, now condemned government intervention, while the Jeffersonian constituency, the plain people, once the advocate of a weak central government and of states' rights, now favored government intervention.

In the 1980s, with the presidency of Ronald Reagan, the debate has burst out with unusual intensity. According to conservatives, government intervention abridges liberty, stifles enterprise, and is inefficient, wasteful, and arbitrary. It disturbs the harmony of the self-adjusting market and creates worse troubles than it solves. Get government off our backs, according to the popular cliché, and our problems will solve themselves. When government is necessary, let it be at the local level, close to the people. Above all, stop the inexorable growth of the federal government.

In fact, for all the talk about the "swollen" and "bloated" bureaucracy, the federal establishment has not been growing as inexorably as many Americans seem to believe. In 1949, it consisted of 2.1 million people. Thirty years later, while the country had grown by 70 million, the federal force had grown only by 750,000. Federal workers were a smaller percentage of the population in 1985 than they were in 1955—or in 1940. The federal establishment, in short, has not kept pace with population growth. Moreover, national defense and the postal service account for 60 percent of federal employment.

Why then the widespread idea about the remorseless growth of government? It is partly because in the 1960s the national government assumed new and intrusive functions: affirmative action in civil rights, environmental protection, safety and health in the workplace, community organization, legal aid to the poor. Although this enlargement of the federal regulatory role was accompanied by marked growth in the size of government on all levels, the expansion has taken place primarily in state and local government. Whereas the federal force increased by only 27 percent in the 30 years after 1950, the state and local government force increased by an astonishing 212 percent.

Despite the statistics, the conviction flourishes in some minds that the national government is a steadily growing behemoth swallowing up the liberties of the people. The foes of Washington prefer local government, feeling it is closer to the people and therefore allegedly more responsive to popular needs. Obviously there is a great deal to be said for settling local questions locally. But local government is characteristically the government of the locally powerful. Historically, the way the locally powerless have won their human and constitutional rights has often been through appeal to the national government. The national government has vindicated racial justice against local bigotry, defended the Bill of Rights against local vigilantism, and protected natural resources against local greed. It has civilized industry and secured the rights of labor organizations. Had the states' rights creed prevailed, there would perhaps still be slavery in the United States.

The national authority, far from diminishing the individual, has given most Americans more personal dignity and liberty than ever before. The individual freedoms destroyed by the increase in national authority have been in the main the freedom to deny black Americans their rights as citizens; the freedom to put small children to work in mills and immigrants in sweatshops; the freedom to pay starvation wages, require barbarous working hours, and permit squalid working conditions; the freedom to deceive in the sale of goods and securities; the freedom to pollute the environment—all freedoms that, one supposes, a civilized nation can readily do without.

"Statements are made," said President John F. Kennedy in 1963, "labelling the Federal Government an outsider, an intruder, an adversary. . . . The United States Government is not a stranger or not an enemy. It is the people of fifty states joining in a national effort. . . . Only a great national effort by a great people working together can explore the mysteries of space, harvest the products at the bottom of the ocean, and mobilize the human, natural, and material resources of our lands."

So an old debate continues. However, Americans are of two minds. When pollsters ask large, spacious questions—Do you think government has become too involved in your lives? Do you think government should stop regulating business?—a sizable majority opposes big government. But when asked specific questions about the practical work of government—Do you favor social security? unemployment compensation? Medicare? health and safety standards in factories? environmental protection? government guarantee of jobs for everyone seeking employment? price and wage controls when inflation threatens?—a sizable majority approves of intervention.

In general, Americans do not want less government. What they want is more efficient government. They want government to do a better job. For a time in the 1970s, with Vietnam and Watergate, Americans lost confidence in the national government. In 1964, more than three-quarters of those polled had thought the national government could be trusted to do right most of the time. By 1980 only one-quarter was prepared to offer such trust. But by 1984 trust in the federal government to manage national affairs had climbed back to 45 percent.

Bureaucracy is a term of abuse. But it is impossible to run any large organization, whether public or private, without a bureaucracy's division of labor and hierarchy of authority. And we live in a world of large organizations. Without bureaucracy modern society would collapse. The problem is not to abolish bureaucracy, but to make it flexible, efficient, and capable of innovation.

Two hundred years after the drafting of the Constitution, Americans still regard government with a mixture of reliance and mistrust—a good combination. Mistrust is the best way to keep government reliable. Informed criticism

12

is the means of correcting governmental inefficiency, incompetence, and arbitrariness; that is, of best enabling government to play its essential role. For without government, we cannot attain the goals of the Founding Fathers. Without an understanding of government, we cannot have the informed criticism that makes government do the job right. It is the duty of every American citizen to know our government—which is what this series is all about.

A survivor of the 1980 fire aboard the Prinsendam *heads for shore in Sitka, Alaska, wearing clothing provided by the Coast Guard. Coast Guard helicopters, aided by U.S. Air Force and Canadian craft, rescued all of the* Prinsendam's *passengers and crew before fire destroyed the ship.*

ONE

Always Ready

For the 320 passengers aboard the cruise ship *Prinsendam*, the monthlong cruise from Vancouver, Canada, to the Asian island of Singapore in October 1980 was the luxurious fulfillment of a dream. As the 426-foot-long, $27-million ship, built just 7 years earlier, steamed through the chilly Gulf of Alaska, they lined the rails to watch whales spouting by day and northern lights glimmering by night. Most of the passengers had retired to their staterooms when, early one stormy morning, an accident below deck swiftly turned the dream into a nightmare.

No one is sure exactly how the accident happened, but it is likely that a broken fuel line sprayed diesel fuel onto hot pipes, where it burst into flames. The resulting fire destroyed the ship's electrical system—including its sophisticated electronic fire-fighting devices. Crewmen with hand-held fire extinguishers could not control the blaze. At 1:30 A.M., the passengers—many of them elderly people, clad in bathrobes and slippers—were called onto the decks. There they huddled in confusion while the ship's chorus tried to keep up their spirits with songs from Broadway musicals, and the captain and crew fought desperately below to save the ship.

Almost five hours later, the captain knew that they had lost the fight. He gave the order to abandon ship. All of the passengers and the 200 crew members got into lifeboats. Safely launched into heavy seas and tossed about by 25-foot waves, the boats huddled in a ragged flotilla near their mother ship, which was tilting badly in the water and pouring forth clouds of dark smoke.

15

The fire-gutted **Prinsendam.** *The ship sank a week after the Coast Guard's heroic rescue of its 520 passengers and crew.*

Soaked with icy spray, shivering with cold and fear, and groaning with seasickness, some of the passengers bravely struck up a round of "Row, Row, Row Your Boat." They were 200 miles from land.

Fortunately for the beleaguered vacationers and crew, help was on the way. Radio distress signals had gone out from the *Prinsendam* as soon as the fire started. By the time the first lifeboats were lowered into the water, three vessels of the United States Coast Guard and one U.S. supertanker, the *Williamsburgh*, were making their best speed toward the stricken ship. By 9:30 A.M., helicopters from the rescue craft had begun lifting people out of the lifeboats in baskets and ferrying them to the waiting ships. Battling high winds and heavy seas, the experienced crews of four Coast Guard helicopters, aided by one chopper from the U.S. Air Force and two from Canada, managed to bring up every one of the *Prinsendam*'s passengers and crew before nightfall. A medic with one of the rescue teams said, "Eight hours later, we would have lost half of them." The 520 survivors were brought ashore at Sitka, Alaska;

many wore sweatshirts or blankets marked "U.S. Coast Guard." The *Prinsendam*, still burning, sank a week later.

The rescue of the *Prinsendam* survivors is a good example of what most people imagine when they think of the United States Coast Guard: saving lives at sea. Search-and-rescue operations, however, constitute just one of many Coast Guard responsibilities. Although the Coast Guard is the smallest of the U.S. armed forces, with a total of 38,500 officers and enlisted men and women, it may also be the most versatile. Its motto is the Latin *Semper Paratus*, which means "Always Ready," and the Coast Guard has always been ready to do any of a multitude of jobs—from cleaning up an oil spill in San Francisco to battling drug smugglers in the Straits of Florida to patrolling the coasts of Southeast Asia during the Vietnam War. In carrying out their duties, the people of the Coast Guard have herded caribou, lassoed icebergs, lived in lonely lighthouses, scrubbed pelicans, learned to handle every form of transportation from the horse to the helicopter, saved countless lives and billions of dollars' worth of property, and fought and died in every U.S. war since the American Revolution.

U.S. Coast Guard crews raise a Viet Cong junk they sank in the Gulf of Thailand in September 1965. During the Vietnam War, as in all other U.S. wars, the Coast Guard acted as a military backup for the U.S. Navy.

Although the Coast Guard acquired its present name in 1915, it originated more than a century earlier, in the first days of the United States. Initially, the service was a branch of the Treasury Department. It was the creation of Alexander Hamilton, the first U.S. secretary of the Treasury, and its purpose was to boost the young nation's sagging finances by enforcing the tariff laws, which required shippers to pay a tax to the government when goods were brought into or taken out of the country. This task was best carried out in U.S. coastal waters and ports, so the new service consisted of ships and sailors; it was a maritime force—one concerned with the sea and shipping—from the start. And less than a decade after its founding, Hamilton's Treasury fleet began fighting the French on the high seas. It had become, as it remains today, one of the nation's armed forces.

Over time, the service's responsibilities and activities changed and expanded in response to special problems and new technology. The development of steam power and the growth of steamboat traffic on the nation's waterways, for example, resulted in several tragic ship explosions in the mid-1800s; these disasters in turn led Congress to establish a steamboat inspection service. Similarly, the loss of the luxury liner *Titanic* in 1912, after it collided with an iceberg in the North Atlantic, brought about the founding of the International Ice Patrol. These and many other duties, including lighthouse maintenance, lifesaving services, and environmental protection, were gradually added to the original tariff-enforcing service to form the modern, multipurpose Coast Guard.

For 177 years after its founding, the Coast Guard remained part of the Treasury Department. In 1967, the Coast Guard was transferred to the newly created Department of Transportation (DOT). Today it operates as part of the DOT, with headquarters in Washington, D.C. Yet the Coast Guard is also, according to Title 14 of the United States Code, "at all times an Armed Force of the United States." It is considered as much a part of the nation's military establishment as the army, navy, air force, and Marine Corps. In time of war, or at other times upon the order of the president, the Coast Guard becomes a branch of the U.S. Navy. It was transferred temporarily to the Navy Department from 1917 to 1919, during World War I, and again from 1941 to 1945, during World War II. The Coast Guard has taken part in all other U.S. conflicts as well, from the War of 1812 to the Vietnam War, although it was not always officially transferred to the navy during these crises.

Today's Coast Guard is the product of two centuries of change and growth, during which its original core—the Treasury Department's small fleet of tariff enforcers—has taken on additional duties and has been merged with other organizations. It is chiefly active in U.S. coastal waters up to 200 miles

A Coast Guard icebreaker. Such vessels are built of reinforced steel, which enables them to forge paths through frozen sea-lanes for commercial and military ships.

offshore, but its jurisdiction also covers the nation's inland waterways, the high seas or international waters, and U.S. bases everywhere from the Arctic Ocean at the top of the world to the Antarctic at the bottom. The Coast Guard's current activities are divided into three broad categories, or missions: maritime safety, maritime law enforcement, and military readiness.

Maritime safety, or the safeguarding of lives and property at sea, is carried out through a number of specific programs, including search and rescue, boating safety, aids to navigation, and marine science. The Coast Guard's maritime law-enforcement duties are divided into two categories: enforcing laws that relate to navigation, commercial shipping, and recreational boating, for which the Coast Guard has direct responsibility; and enforcing all U.S. laws at sea, including customs and tariffs—the Coast Guard's original mission—as well as quarantine (holding in isolation offshore an arriving ship suspected of carrying a contagious disease), immigration, smuggling, protection of marine life and the environment, and all federal criminal statutes. In short, if a law can be broken on the water, the Coast Guard is charged with seeing that it is not. The Guard often teams up with other organizations, such as local police forces or the Drug Enforcement Administration (an agency of the Justice Department), in carrying out this part of its mission.

The Coast Guard's third mission is military readiness—being prepared at all times to contribute to national defense. In peacetime, this translates into planning and training for special missions in coastal waters and for the defense of the nation's ports and coastlines in a military emergency.

The Coast Guard may appear small compared to the U.S. Navy, but its 250 large ships and 2,000 smaller craft make it the world's 12th largest naval fleet;

A coastguardsman tosses a life preserver to a downed boater off the Florida coast. Such rescue missions are typical of the Coast Guard's maritime safety duties.

A Coast Guard base on Kodiak Island near Alaska. The Coast Guard owns 205 helicopters and airplanes, in addition to its naval fleet, making it the world's 7th largest naval air force.

it is also the 7th largest naval air force, with 205 helicopters and airplanes. Many seafaring countries—including Great Britain, Canada, and Japan—have services especially assigned to coastal law enforcement and safety. The U.S. Coast Guard is the largest such service in the world. It has saved many thousands of lives that were in peril on the sea and, indirectly, touches the lives of all Americans through law enforcement, safety inspection, and scientific research. The Coast Guard has changed a great deal since its early days as a handful of seagoing tax police, and the process of change is still going on today.

In 1789, Secretary of the Treasury Alexander Hamilton proposed an idea that was the genesis of the Coast Guard. Hamilton envisioned a fleet of small boats to battle smuggling and enforce U.S. tariff laws.

TWO

Born with the Nation

By 1789, the former British colonies of North America had become the United States of America, and the Americans had elected their first president. Despite their newfound independence, however, their troubles were far from over. The new nation faced many problems. One of the most pressing of these was financial. The United States owed $50 million to other countries, and it desperately needed to develop new sources of income. One of the first steps Congress took to solve this problem was the Tariff Act, which was designed to raise money on goods passing into and out of the country.

Tariffs, also called customs duties, are taxes paid on imported goods and, sometimes, on exported goods as well. The shipper or merchant pays the tariff, which is ultimately passed along to the consumer in the form of a higher purchase price. Tariffs are a basic source of income for all nations engaged in commerce; they can be particularly important to a young country with few factories and skilled craftsmen, because so many goods must be brought from outside. Congress was correct in thinking that tariffs would generate a respectable income for the U.S. government.

Taxes are never popular with the general public, however, and the 1789 Tariff Act was especially unpopular with Americans because of the nation's recent history. The colonists had complained long and bitterly about taxes

23

In 1773, angry colonists disguised as Indians raided British ships and dumped cargoes of tea into Boston Harbor to protest unfair taxation. The Boston Tea Party was a major event in the American fight for independence; after the American Revolution, tariffs imposed on the infant nation by its own government caused similar protests.

imposed on them by the British Parliament; in fact, unfair taxation was one of the chief causes of their rebellion. During the years leading up to the American Revolution, many Americans had taken great pride in thwarting Parliament and King George III by smuggling—that is, bringing in goods without paying the tariffs. Boatmen landed in secluded coves far from the prying eyes of port officials, and merchandise such as wine, sugar, paper, and tea entered a great number of colonial homes by way of backwoods trails and hidden warehouses. In those years, smuggling was regarded by many as noble, even patriotic, and the purchase of contraband (smuggled goods) was widespread and almost respectable. But after the Revolution, Congress suddenly found itself in the uncomfortable position of having to enforce tariffs rather than evade them. And there were many Americans who were no more willing to pay Congress's tariffs than they had been to pay King George's. For many smugglers, business continued as usual.

Alexander Hamilton, President George Washington's secretary of the Treasury, knew that unless something was done to control smuggling, the new laws that governed commerce and tariffs would become a useless farce. No sooner had Congress passed the Tariff Act than he made a proposal that was the genesis of the Coast Guard.

The Revenue Marine

Hamilton recommended that the government build a fleet of boats to crack down on smuggling and help collect the revenue from customs duties. He asked for 10 boats to patrol the coastal waters from Maine to Georgia. The boats would be cutters—small ships designed for swift, easy maneuverability in shallow waters, less heavily armed than naval craft and far less bulky than

The Massachusetts, *the first and largest of the original 10 cutters used by the Treasury Department's new Revenue Marine service to patrol coastal waters from Maine to Georgia.*

cargo-carrying merchantmen. (Coast Guard vessels today are designed for the same purposes and are still called cutters.) Hamilton's request was granted, and the cutters were built for the Treasury Department's new service, which was called the Revenue Marine. The first and largest of the original 10 cutters, the *Massachusetts*, was launched in 1791.

Like many federal projects, the *Massachusetts* and her sister ships ultimately cost more than the $1,000 that had been budgeted for each of them, but it seems that they quickly proved their value. No official records survive to tell how many smugglers were captured in the early days of the Revenue Marine, or how much revenue was saved, but it is known that the yearly value of American trade rose from $52 million to $205 million in the first decade of the service's operation. Congress must have believed that the revenue cutters were responsible for at least some of that increase, because in 1793 and 1796 it authorized pay raises for the ships' 80 crewmen.

Little is known about the officers and crewmen of the early Revenue Marine. Some of the captains were veterans of the Continental navy, which had been disbanded after the revolutionary war. President Washington commissioned them as Revenue Marine officers; the signed commission of one of them, Hopley Yeaton of the cutter *Scammel*, has been preserved. Another old document tells the sad story of the third mate of the *Massachusetts*, who was dismissed for speaking rudely to his senior officers and for "keeping bad women on board the Cutter in Boston." For the most part, however, the men of the Revenue Marine seem to have been worthy and competent. And before the decade was out, they proved themselves under fire.

These were years of great hostility among the vessels of France, Great Britain, and the United States. The three nations were vying for control of territory in North America and arguing over trade rights. Although relations never deteriorated into declared warfare, ships of each country chased, attacked, and seized those of the others. By the end of the 1790s, the United States and France were nearly at war on the sea. In 1799, Congress authorized President John Adams to assign the cutters of the Revenue Marine to full combat duty in cooperation with the U.S. Navy, which had been created the year before. This was the beginning of the relationship that exists between the navy and the Coast Guard to this day. Some of the cutters left their coastal stations for the waters of the West Indies, where they were charged with protecting U.S. merchant ships in the sugar and rum trade.

From 1799 to 1800—when Adams and Napoleon Bonaparte of France signed a treaty that ended the naval skirmishing—the revenue cutters captured 16 enemy ships. The *Eagle* took five of these vessels, in addition to recapturing

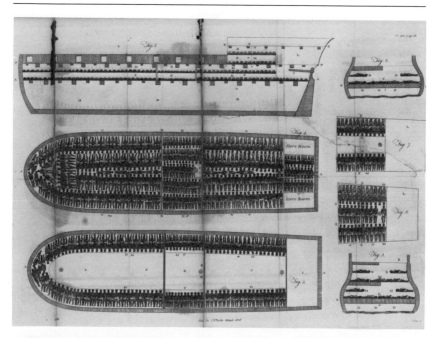

A diagram of a typical 19th-century slave ship. After Congress out-lawed the importation of slaves from Africa in 1807, the Revenue Marine was given the responsibility of enforcing the ban.

seven American ships that had been seized by the French. The 70-man crew of the *Pickering*, on 2 cruises to the West Indies, captured 10 French craft, including a ship that had a crew of more than 200. Although it proved victorious over this well-armed foe, the *Pickering* could not withstand a storm at sea; it sank with all hands in 1800.

In the early 1800s, having proved its value as a military resource, the Revenue Marine returned to its original job of protecting commerce. By this time, the question of slavery had begun to torment the new nation. In 1807, Congress forbade the importation of slaves into the United States on or after January 1, 1808, and charged the Revenue Marine with enforcing this ban. Revenue cutters chased suspected slave ships and, when they caught a slaver, arrested the ship's captain and crew. They then released the ship's human cargo; these captives were given "free" status in the North, which usually meant that they became indentured servants. Also in 1807, President Thomas Jefferson imposed an embargo—a total ban on all shipments of goods into or out of the United States. Jefferson hoped that the trade embargo would force

27

Britain and France to recognize the neutrality of American shipping and stop molesting U.S. vessels. The embargo failed to achieve this and, because it brought economic hardship to many Americans, was extremely unpopular. Equally unpopular were the Revenue Marine men who patrolled the coasts to enforce the embargo. It was not to be the last time that the Coast Guard would carry out its duties in the face of disapproval and resentment from the public.

The embargo ended after 14 months, but the work of the Revenue Marine continued with 12 new cutters. With a total of 16 vessels and the responsibility for patrolling the American coastline from Canada to the West Indies, the service had its work cut out. Soon, however, the service returned to military status when the long-simmering hostility between the United States and Great Britain boiled over in the War of 1812. Some of the Revenue Marine's cutters were assigned to serve with the navy during the war. Less than a week into the conflict, the cutter *Jefferson* captured the first British ship; other cutters also took part in notable and heroic actions. Perhaps the most dramatic incident of the War of 1812 concerned the cutter *Eagle*, which was attacked by the powerfully armed British *Dispatch* in Long Island Sound. The captain of the *Eagle* ran the cutter ashore and ordered his men to carry its guns to the top of a steep hill. From there they fired down on the *Dispatch* until they ran out of ammunition. Several times, men ran down to the beached cutter, under heavy fire, to replace a flag that had been destroyed by enemy bullets and to bring up a new store of ammunition. Not until the men of the *Eagle* had resorted to using the torn-up logbook of the cutter as paper wadding for their muskets were they captured by the British.

After the war ended in 1814, the Revenue Marine faced a new enemy: pirates, especially in the Gulf of Mexico. In 1819, the cutters *Alabama* and *Louisiana* fought and captured the black-flagged *Bravo*, which was commanded by John La Farge, a crony of the notorious pirate Jean Lafitte of New Orleans. Revenue Marine men from these two cutters stormed and wiped out Patterson's Town, a pirate stronghold on an island near the mouth of the Mississippi River. The *Louisiana* captured four pirate ships in the Caribbean in 1822, along with—as her captain, John Lewis, proudly wrote—"$4,000 worth of dry goods which they have robbed and were endeavoring to smuggle into the United States."

Action in the South

The 1830s and 1840s were eventful years for the service. In 1832, five cutters were ordered to Charleston Harbor after South Carolina announced that it

Jean Lafitte, a dreaded 19th-century pirate and smuggler from New Orleans. After the War of 1812, the Revenue Marine clashed with a new enemy when it began battling pirates.

would no longer obey the federal tariff laws. Revenue Marine officers boarded all incoming ships and took custody of their cargoes—by force when necessary—until the required tariffs were paid. The following year, Congress passed a new tariff act, a compromise between the original act and South Carolina's demands. The 1833 act lowered some tariffs and helped to restore peace between the rebellious state and the federal government.

Farther south, in Florida, the Seminole Indians were violently resisting attempts to relocate them farther west in order to free up their land for white settlers. During the Seminole wars of 1836 to 1839, the Seminole, who lived deep in the swamps and along rivers, fought off army and navy forces; the Revenue Marine, which was experienced in navigating rivers, inlets, and shallow waters, helped transport federal troops and supplies, blockade Indian settlements, and protect white settlements. Revenue mariners also took part, occasionally, in land battles against the Seminole. A decade later, during the Mexican War, when the navy needed small ships for use in the coastal waters off Mexico, the Revenue Marine pitched in with nine cutters and their crews. It was now clear that this small fleet, which had begun as a tax enforcer, possessed great skill in what was called "brown-water" warfare—navigating

Indians attack a ship in Florida during the Seminole wars of 1836–39. During this conflict, the Revenue Marine transported army and navy troops and supplies through the narrow rivers and swamps of the South.

and fighting in shallow, often dangerous, coastal waters (as opposed to the "blue-water" warfare of the open seas).

By this time, the service had a new, more formal organizational structure. For its first five decades, it had been administered piecemeal by the customs collectors of the various ports, under the loose supervision of the secretary of the Treasury. In 1843, the Treasury Department established the Revenue Marine Bureau in Washington; the bureau was headed by Alexander Fraser, an experienced cutter captain who was determined to streamline and unify the administration of the service. In 1844, Fraser began issuing official annual reports on the service's status and plans. Under his leadership, the service experimented with steam-powered craft in the late 1840s, but the experiment was not a success: Six steam cutters proved slow, leaky, and inefficient. By 1849, the Revenue Marine had returned to familiar, dependable sail.

New Coasts and Conflicts

The Revenue Marine had been born with the United States. During the second half of the 19th century, the service grew and changed as the nation expanded. As states were formed from the Northwest Territory (the area presently

In 1848 (top), San Francisco was a sleepy port town; by 1850 (bottom), after gold was discovered in the region, fortune seekers had flooded the harbor and its surrounding hillsides.

occupied by Ohio, Indiana, Illinois, Michigan, Wisconsin, and part of Minnesota) and the Louisiana Purchase (land bought from France in 1803 that doubled the size of the United States and later formed Arkansas, Iowa, Missouri, Nebraska, and parts of nine other states), settlement of these new areas increased traffic on the Great Lakes and the Mississippi River. These regions did not immediately fall under the jurisdiction of the Revenue Marine, but they would have a tremendous effect on the service in years to come.

Of more immediate impact was the acquisition of Washington and Oregon from Britain in 1846 and California from Mexico in 1848 (these territories would be admitted to the Union as states in 1889, 1859, and 1850, respectively). Suddenly, the coastline of the United States—and the territory that had to be patrolled by the Revenue Marine—was doubled. During the hectic first months of the 1849 California gold rush, when San Francisco became almost overnight one of the world's busiest ports, the revenue cutter *Lawrence*—under the command of Captain Fraser, who had left his desk job after five years—was the only federal muscle on hand to enforce the tariff laws and keep order in the city's crowded harbor and waterfront. To the north, along Puget Sound in Washington, the Revenue Marine helped the army subdue an Indian uprising in 1855. And far to the south, the revenue cutter *Harriet Lane*, the service's first successful steam-powered vessel, was part of a navy squadron that the United States sent to South America in 1858 to show North American strength after Paraguayan forces fired on a U.S. ship bound for exploration of that country's rivers.

A year or two later, the Revenue Marine had plenty to do much closer to home. As North and South drifted toward Civil War, the service found itself, like the nation, divided in its loyalties. In January 1861, Treasury Secretary John A. Dix feared losing control of the cutter *McClelland*, which was then posted at New Orleans. The cutter's captain was known to have Southern sympathies, and Dix feared that he might turn the vessel over to the Confederacy. "If any one attempts to haul down the American flag," Dix telegraphed to the cutter's second-in-command, "shoot him on the spot." Despite this stern order, Captain John G. Brushwood survived to turn the *McClelland* over to the South; however, many crew members of several cutters that were seized by the South remained loyal to the North and eventually made their way overland to Union lines.

Twenty-eight cutters remained with the Union. In addition, Northern forces purchased—or, in some cases, received donation of—several yachts and ships from patriotic Northerners. The Revenue Marine was involved in all phases of the conflict. Its chief duty was to blockade Southern ports so that supplies

Treasury Department)
Jan. 29, 1861

Tell Lieut. Caldwell to arrest Capt. Breshwood, assume command of the Cutter and obey the order I gave through you. If Capt. Breshwood after arrest undertakes to interfere with the command of the Cutter, tell Lieut. Caldwell to consider him as a mutineer & treat him accordingly. If any one attempts to haul down the American flag, shoot him on the spot. —

John A. Dix
Secretary of the Treasury.

Treasury Secretary John A. Dix dispatched this order to prevent the southern-born captain of the McClelland from surrendering his ship to the Confederacy: "If anyone attempts to haul down the American flag, shoot him on the spot."

A Revenue Marine cutter chases down a blockade-runner during the Civil War. The Revenue Marine was in charge of blockading Southern ports so that supplies could not get through.

could not get through. But the service also saw combat and a number of special assignments. The *Harriet Lane*, under Union command, was the first ship to fire a shot in the Civil War; posted at the entrance to Charleston Harbor while Fort Sumter was under attack by Confederate cannon, the *Harriet Lane* fired a shot across the bow of a ship that tried to enter the harbor without raising a flag to show which side it was on. The *Miami* carried President Abraham Lincoln on a secret visit to Confederate-held territory in Virginia to examine a potential landing spot for Union troops. The *Caleb Cushing* was captured by Confederate raiders in Portland, Maine, and then recaptured by the Portland customs collectors. The *Harriet Lane*, after leaving Charleston, helped capture Fort Hatteras and then served as the flagship of Union admiral David Porter. It was captured by the Confederates in 1863 and was part of the Southern fleet for the rest of the war. Revenue cutters engaged in combat with the Confederate navy in Chesapeake Bay and the waters off the Carolinas.

When the war ended in 1865, the Revenue Marine resumed its peacetime job of tariff protection. But almost at once its responsibilities grew again. In 1867, the United States purchased the Alaska territory from Russia, and the Revenue Marine acquired thousands of miles of additional coastline to patrol. For some years afterward, the Revenue Marine and a handful of army troops were the only military and legal representatives of the U.S. government in Alaska. The officers and men of the revenue cutters were called upon to do everything from performing marriages for the Alaskan natives to exploring rivers in animal-skin boats to collecting specimens of animals and plants for the Smithsonian Institution (a museum and educational and research center established in Washington, D.C., in 1846 to house U.S. cultural, historical, and scientific collections). Cutters carried doctors and medicine to the sick, brought provisions to native communities that were low on food, and made

The Harriet Lane, *the Revenue Marine's first successful steam powered cutter, helped to show U.S. strength in a confrontation with Paraguay in 1858. Three years later it was the first ship to fire a shot in the Civil War.*

The Polar *Bear*

The *Bear* was built in Scotland in 1874 for the sealing trade in the North Atlantic waters between Newfoundland and Greenland, and its hull was specially strengthened to sail in seas thick with pounding, grinding ice. For a decade the vessel's bloody-handed crew slaughtered thousands of seals each year for their fur. The carved wooden figurehead of the ship *Bear* was a snarling, rearing polar bear—a fitting symbol for the devastation it brought to the seal colonies.

In 1884, the U.S. Navy bought the *Bear* and sent it into the little-known region far above the Arctic Circle to rescue Lieutenant Adolphus Greeley, who had been lost for three years on an expedition in the Arctic. This mission of mercy—Greeley and five of his men were finally brought back alive—was the beginning of the *Bear*'s long career of government service in the polar seas.

The Revenue Marine acquired the ship in 1885 and sent it to Alaska to prevent poaching in the seal colonies of the Pribilof Islands. Once a sealer itself, the *Bear* was now the representative of law and order; over the years, its captains arrested hundreds of seal poachers from all nations. The *Bear* also carried mail and emergency provisions, quelled at least two mutinies on whaling vessels, rescued dozens of stranded or shipwrecked sailors from the coasts of Alaska and Russia, tried to prevent the smuggling of liquor and firearms to the Eskimos, and generally did whatever needed to be done.

For the first few years, the *Bear* was one of only three cutters responsible for keeping the peace on the lawless Alaskan frontier. Then, in the mid-1890s, the Revenue Marine sent additional cutters north to form the Bering Sea Patrol. As a member of this force, the *Bear* led one of the most adventurous rescues in Coast Guard history. In the fall of 1897, just as severe weather set in, the *Bear*'s captain received word that 8 whaling ships, with more than 300 crewmen, were frozen in the ice near Point Barrow on Alaska's north coast and did not have enough food for the winter. Although the *Bear* had just docked in Seattle for the winter, it at once set off for the Arctic Ocean—something that had never before been done in winter. Pack ice kept the *Bear* from reaching Point Barrow, so three crewmen set off overland with guides and dogsleds. They rounded up a herd of 400 reindeer; then, overcoming tremendous cold and fatigue, they drove the herd north for 2,000 miles and more than 3 months until they reached Point Barrow. The reindeer kept the starving men alive until the ice broke up and the ships could leave. The three men received gold medals from Congress for their heroism; one of them was Ellsworth Bertholf, who later became the first commandant of the U.S. Coast Guard.

After 40 years in the North Pacific, the *Bear* was retired from Coast Guard service in 1926. It was sent to Oakland, California, to be used as a museum. A film company borrowed the ship for a movie based on Jack London's *The Sea Wolf*. It seemed that the *Bear*'s career on the high seas had ended.

But Admiral Richard E. Byrd had other ideas. He needed ships for a second expedition to Antarctica, and he bought the old ice ship *Bear* for $1,500, refitting it for the voyage. In 1933, the vessel set off for Little America, Byrd's Antarctic base, to battle the ice of the southern polar sea. When he returned home in 1935, even Byrd felt that the *Bear* had earned a final retirement. He

donated its famous figurehead to the Mariner's Museum in Newport News, Virginia.

In 1940, international conflict called the *Bear* back to duty. With World War II looming on the horizon, Byrd was asked to return to Little America to keep Hitler's Germany from claiming Antarctic territory, so he took the *Bear* south again. Then, when the United States entered the war in 1941, the ship was brought north to serve in the Northeast Greenland Patrol, a fleet that patrolled the western North Atlantic for German weather stations, submarines, and secret radio bases. After many years, the *Bear* was back in the waters it had first known as a sealer. It even made the headlines for towing the *Buskoe*, the first enemy vessel captured by the United States in World War II, into Boston harbor in October 1941.

But the *Bear*'s years of glory and service ended with the war. In 1944, after 70 years in the polar seas, it was sent to a salvage yard. A sealer from Nova Scotia bought the boat, hoping to return it to its original trade, but he could not afford the refitting costs. Years later, a restaurant owner bought the *Bear*. He planned to tow it from Nova Scotia and turn it into a waterfront restaurant in Philadelphia, but his plan failed. The vessel took on water in a heavy storm and had to be abandoned. On March 19, 1963, the ice ship *Bear* sank 90 miles south of Nova Scotia, not far from the sealing grounds it had entered 89 years before.

The Revenue Marine cutter Hudson *tows the damaged U.S. Navy torpedo boat* Winslow *to safety in Cárdenas Bay, Cuba, in May 1898. After the conclusion of the Spanish-American War, the captain and crew of the* Hudson *received congressional Medals of Honor for this act of bravery.*

dangerous voyages across the Bering Sea to Siberia, in Russia, to buy extra-hardy reindeer to improve the Alaskan herds. In the 1890s, the Revenue Marine Bureau formally organized the cutters of the North Pacific into the Bering Sea Patrol.

In 1898, the Revenue Marine found itself once again embroiled in war. The Spanish-American War pitted the United States against Spain in the Philippines and Cuba. Fighting thus occurred in two places: in the Pacific Ocean, far south of the Bering Sea, and in the Caribbean, close to the southern shores of the United States. The cutter *McCulloch* was dispatched to the Philippines, where it helped Commodore George Dewey's squadron destroy the Spanish fleet at the Battle of Manila Bay. Meanwhile, on the other side of the world, eight cutters—some of them drawn from the Bering Sea Patrol—helped blockade the Cuban port of Havana, and the cutter *Hudson* joined the U.S. Navy blockade of Cárdenas Bay. When the navy's torpedo boat *Winslow* was struck by shells in Cárdenas Bay and began drifting toward shore, the *Hudson* braved shallow water and enemy fire to tow the

Winslow to safety. After the war, the cutter's captain and crew received congressional Medals of Honor.

The Revenue Marine ended the 19th century on this heroic note. During its first century, it had demonstrated fortitude and versatility; it had expanded to many times its original size; and its activities had gone far beyond what had originally been envisioned by Hamilton and Congress. It also had a new name—around the turn of the century, the Revenue Marine officially became the Revenue Cutter Service. Its second century was to be a time of even greater expansion and versatility, in which the service would be tested repeatedly at home and abroad, would acquire new responsibilities, and would become the U.S. Coast Guard.

The Boston Light Station, America's oldest and most famous lighthouse, was built in 1716. First the responsibility of the individual colonies and later of the Lighthouse Service, lighthouse construction and maintenance duties were given to the Coast Guard in 1939.

THREE

A New Era

In the early years of the 20th century, the Revenue Cutter Service came under scrutiny from critics who questioned its value. Its original mission—to enforce the tariff laws and prevent smuggling—was no longer urgent. Some people thought these tasks could be handled by local police, the customs offices, and the navy. It was said that the navy also could take over the duties that the Revenue Cutter Service had performed during wartime. A commission on federal economy appointed by President William Howard Taft reported in 1911 that the revenue service "has not a single duty or function that cannot be performed by some other existing service . . . at much smaller expense."

The commandant of the service at this time was Captain Ellsworth P. Bertholf, who had served in the Bering Sea Patrol. As might be expected, his views on the matter differed quite strongly from those of the commission, and he argued forcefully for the continuation of the service. Treasury Secretary Franklin MacVeagh echoed Bertholf's opinion, saying, "The service is at the highest point of its 120 years." Eventually, he and Bertholf carried the day, and the service was not discontinued. In the interests of economy and efficiency, however, it was reorganized.

In fact, the revenue service has undergone three major reorganizations since Bertholf's day. In each case, it either absorbed or was merged with another federal service. The three agencies that thus became a part of the revenue service were the Lifesaving Service, the Lighthouse Service, and the Bureau of Navigation and Steamboat Inspection Service. Each of these brought its own history and special functions to the united service.

Added in 1915: The Lifesaving Service

The first and most thoroughgoing reorganization involved the Lifesaving Service, which already had a history half as long as that of the Revenue Cutter Service. The revenue service itself had engaged in some early lifesaving work as far back as 1831, when cutter captains in treacherous waters were ordered to patrol for vessels in distress and help them when possible. Before long, however, it became clear that this informal approach was not enough. The number of shipwrecks in U.S. coastal waters increased in the mid-19th century as commerce boomed and crowded ships full of immigrants set sail for American ports, especially New York. It was common during the winter months for storms from the northeast to drive these vessels onto sandbars off the New Jersey shore. Rescue attempts from shore were successful only about half of the time. New equipment, techniques, and organization were needed to save the growing number of lives in peril off the coast.

Around 1848, the Treasury Department began forming a federally funded lifesaving service. Stations were built in areas where wrecks were frequent, such as New Jersey and Long Island. The stations were operated by teams made up of Revenue Marine officers, state or local salvage contractors, and citizen volunteers. They were equipped with surfboats mounted on wagons for quick transfer to wreck sites; ropes; a cannon for firing lines to the ships; stoves; fuel; and a small enclosed car for hauling survivors on a line through pounding surf. Some of these devices were perfected by Joshua James, a famous lifesaver who was so dedicated to his life's work that he was carried to his funeral in a horse-drawn lifeboat. The service immediately demonstrated its value. In 1850, a team of trained volunteers using the new surf car rescued 201 of the 202 passengers of the *Ayrshire*, which ran aground during a snowstorm at Squan Beach, New Jersey.

After the Civil War, the Lifesaving Service expanded rapidly. It was headed by Sumner I. Kimball, former chief of the Revenue Marine Bureau, who has been called the "father of modern lifesaving"; he received help from cutter captain John Faunce, who had fired the historic shot from the *Harriet Lane* at Fort Sumter. Under the guidance of these two men, the Lifesaving Service built many new stations, developed and tested new equipment and methods, and investigated shipwrecks to learn how they could be prevented. The records of successful rescues mounted steadily. In just 3 days in September 1889, crews at 3 Delaware stations helped 22 vessels in distress; they saved 194 lives and did not lose 1. From 1871, when Kimball took over, to 1914, the

Volunteers working under the auspices of the Lifesaving Service haul passengers of the Ayrshire *to safety in a surf car after the ship ran aground on Squan Beach, New Jersey, in an 1850 snowstorm. In 1915, the Lifesaving Service was merged with the Revenue Cutter Service to form the U.S. Coast Guard.*

Lifesaving Service assisted 178,741 people, many of whom were in grave danger.

Each district of the Lifesaving Service reported to a revenue service captain, yet the two organizations remained structurally separate within the Treasury Department. Then, in the aftermath of the 1911 presidential-commission report recommending the discontinuance of the Revenue Cutter Service, a dramatic incident illustrated the value of cooperation between the cutters and lifesavers. A ship called the *Ontario* caught fire off Long Island in April 1912. Still burning, it was guided to shore by two revenue cutters. The crew of the local lifesaving station fought the flames and then, when the fire proved impossible to douse, used their new equipment to rescue some of the crewmen while the cutter crews rescued the others. This act of cooperation may have been in the minds of most members of Congress and President Woodrow Wilson when, three years later, the Revenue Cutter Service and the Lifesaving Service were officially merged—still within the Treasury Department—to form the U.S. Coast Guard.

In 1911 Captain Ellsworth P. Bertholf, a veteran of the Bering Sea Patrol and commandant of the Revenue Cutter Service from 1911–15, argued against charges that the service was obsolete. His efforts secured the continuation of the service.

At its birth, the Coast Guard had 4,155 officers and men, 45 cutters, and 280 lifesaving stations. Captain Bertholf, who had defended the revenue service from the threat of elimination, was made the first Coast Guard commandant.

Added in 1939: The Lighthouse Service

The sea is always potentially dangerous, but never more so, some say, than where it meets the land. Ships that approach land are threatened by sandbars, shallows, rocks, reefs, treacherous currents, or simply the risk of running headlong onto the shore at night. Beacons and bonfires have long been used on hills and highlands to guide ships at night. Lighthouses—towers with lamps—came into wide use in the 18th century.

The Lighthouse Service is the oldest branch of the Coast Guard; it is 60 years older than the Revenue Marine. The first lighthouse in the country was built on Little Brewster Island in the Massachusetts Bay Colony in 1716. For many years, building and operating lighthouses was the responsibility of the individual colonies. In 1789, a year before the founding of the Revenue Marine, Congress assigned responsibility for a nationwide Lighthouse Service to the Treasury Department. The service remained in that department until 1903; at that time, it was transferred to the Department of Commerce and Labor, where it remained until 1939, when it was absorbed by the Coast Guard.

Over the years, lighthouse technology changed enormously. Lamps that were fueled by whale oil in colonial days were later fueled by kerosene and then by electricity. In the 1700s, lighthouse keepers used a cannon when it was foggy to warn ships away; this device was replaced in turn by a mechanical bell,

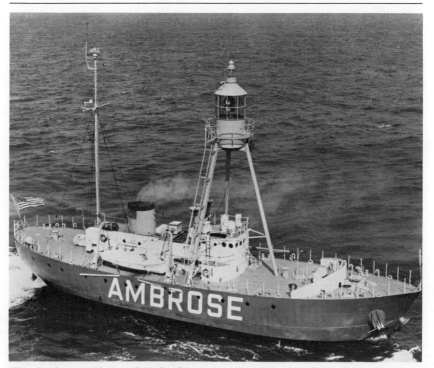

The Ambrose Channel lightship, posted in New York harbor, withstood 4 collisions in 56 years.

45

a foghorn, and an air siren. Starting in 1820, lightships were stationed in hazardous waters in Chesapeake Bay and other places where it was impractical or impossible to build lighthouses; after World War II, the lightships were replaced by automated lights on metal scaffolding grounded deep in the seabed.

Working in the Lighthouse Service was eventful. Dozens of lighthouses were destroyed by storms and hurricanes. In the early days, some lighthouse keepers faced Indian attacks. In the 20th century, a lightship near Nantucket was rammed and destroyed with all hands by the liner *Olympic*, sister ship to the unlucky *Titanic*. The Ambrose Channel lightship in New York harbor was struck 4 times in 56 years. Despite these hardships, the Lighthouse Service was one of the first parts of the federal administration to open career doors to women. Several dozen women operated lighthouses in the 19th century; one of the most famous, Ida Lewis, served as the keeper of Lime Rock lighthouse in Newport Harbor for 32 years. Today, the image of the lonely lighthouse keeper gazing out to sea is a thing of the past—nearly all of the Coast Guard's lighthouses are fully automated, battery-operated, and visited only by maintenance crews.

Added in 1942: The Bureau of Navigation and Steamboat Inspection Service

New technology brings not only advantages but also new risks, as the American people found out during the great steamboat era of the 19th century. Steam engines made passenger and freight traffic on the nation's waterways faster and more profitable than ever; the Mississippi River, in particular, became a grand highway of ever-larger steamboats. But the coal- and wood-fueled boilers of these craft were sensitive and potentially explosive. A series of boiler explosions took many lives, culminating in 1837 in an explosion and fire on the *Pulaski* that killed 100 people.

The public demanded better safety on the waterways, and in 1838 Congress passed an act that created a Steamboat Inspection Service within the Justice Department. Unfortunately, the standards for inspection were rather loose and inconsistent, and enforcement of the act was almost nonexistent. Hazards continued to multiply. Between December 1851 and July 1852, 7 steamboat disasters killed nearly 700 people. A new, stricter act was passed in 1852, and the service was moved to the Treasury Department. In 1903, it was transferred to the Department of Commerce and Labor, and in 1932 it was

Steamboats on the Mississippi River in the 19th century. Although the advent of steam-powered ships made traveling by water more efficient, steam power also proved to be dangerous because boilers were fueled by potentially explosive material. In 1838, Congress created the Steamboat Inspection Service to oversee these sometimes hazardous craft.

combined with the Bureau of Navigation, which was responsible for maintaining aids to navigation—such as buoys and charts—on the nation's waterways. This combined service was absorbed by the Coast Guard in 1942.

Battling Nature and Man

While all of these internal changes were taking place, the Coast Guard continued to be shaped by events in the outside world. One such event in 1912 was an international tragedy. The luxury liner *Titanic*, making its first voyage, struck an iceberg and sank in the North Atlantic before rescue craft could reach it; although many passengers survived in lifeboats, 1,517 people drowned. The danger posed by these gigantic, drifting blocks of ice had become quite grave, and everyone wanted to avoid another iceberg collision. The Revenue Cutter Service began patrolling the most dangerous North Atlantic iceberg zone in

47

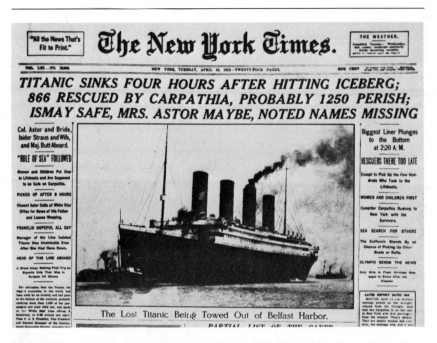

The New York Times.

VOL. LXX...NO. 19,XXX.　　　NEW YORK, TUESDAY, APRIL 16, 1912—TWENTY-FOUR PAGES.　　　ONE CENT

TITANIC SINKS FOUR HOURS AFTER HITTING ICEBERG; 866 RESCUED BY CARPATHIA, PROBABLY 1250 PERISH; ISMAY SAFE, MRS. ASTOR MAYBE, NOTED NAMES MISSING

Col. Astor and Bride, Isidor Straus and Wife, and Maj. Butt Aboard.

"RULE OF SEA" FOLLOWED

Women and Children Put Over in Lifeboats and Are Supposed to be Safe on Carpathia.

PICKED UP AFTER 8 HOURS

Vincent Astor Calls at White Star Office for News of His Father and Leaves Weeping.

FRANKLIN HOPEFUL ALL DAY

Manager of the Line Insisted Titanic Was Unsinkable Even After She Had Gone Down.

HEAD OF THE LINE ABOARD

A Brave Isnay Making First Trip to Organize Only That Was to Surpass All Others.

Biggest Liner Plunges to the Bottom at 2:20 A. M.

RESCUERS THERE TOO LATE

Except to Pick Up the Few Hundreds Who Took to the Lifeboats.

WOMEN AND CHILDREN FIRST

Cunarder Carpathia Rushing to New York with the Survivors.

SEA SEARCH FOR OTHERS

The California Stands By on Chance of Picking Up Other Boats or Rafts.

OLYMPIC SENDS THE NEWS

Only Ship to Flash Wireless Messages to Shore After the Disaster.

LATER REPORT SAVES 866

BOSTON, April 15 —A wireless message picked up late to-night, relayed from the Olympic, says that the Carpathia is on her way to New York with 866 passengers from the steamer Titanic aboard. They are mainly women and children, the message said, and it seem...

The Lost Titanic Being Towed Out of Belfast Harbor.

PARTIAL LIST OF THE SAVED

The 1912 Titanic *disaster stunned the world. The ship, thought to be unsinkable, hit an iceberg and went down in the North Atlantic, taking 1,517 passengers with it.*

1913. The following year, more than a dozen nations that used the North Atlantic shipping routes joined to form the International Ice Patrol. The nations agreed to share the cost of the patrol, each making a contribution in proportion to the amount of shipping it sent through the iceberg zone, and the Revenue Cutter Service was asked to undertake the actual patrol duty. Under a similar financial arrangement, the Coast Guard continues the International Ice Patrol today.

Not long after the commencement of the ice patrol, World War I broke out. When the United States entered the war in 1917, the Coast Guard assumed military duties and became part of the Navy Department for two years. Its cutters and crews were responsible for patrolling Canadian, U.S., and Caribbean coastal waters on the lookout for German submarines. Additionally, a fleet of six cutters was sent to the Atlantic Fleet Patrol in Europe and assigned to convoy duty, shepherding Allied ships through the submarine-infested waters between England and the Mediterranean Sea. One of these cutters, the *Tampa*, disappeared at sea with a crew of 131 in September 1918, just 2 months before the war ended. Only a few scraps of wreckage and two unidentifiable bodies were found. It is probable that the *Tampa*—the Coast Guard's greatest loss of the war—was torpedoed.

After World War I, the Coast Guard faced a new challenge when an old duty—cracking down on smuggling—was revived. In 1920, an amendment to the U.S. Constitution made it illegal for Americans to manufacture, transport, or sell alcoholic beverages. Because these activities were banned, or prohibited, the 13 years that followed came to be called the Prohibition Era. Prohibition was far from universally popular, however, and within a year a multimillion-dollar smuggling network, operated in large part by criminal syndicates, had sprung up to supply illicit liquor to thirsty Americans. Outside the three-mile limit of U.S. territorial waters, fleets of vessels loaded with liquor from Canada, the West Indies, and Europe anchored or drifted off the New Jersey, Long Island, and Massachusetts coasts. Under cover of night, smaller boats would slip out to these "Rum Rows," as they were called, to unload the liquid cargoes.

Called upon to combat smuggling, the Coast Guard kept the Rum Rows under surveillance. It could take no action against the foreign-owned "mother

The Coast Guard cutter Tampa *disappeared at sea in 1918, with all hands. One of the largest U.S. Navy losses of World War I, the* Tampa *is believed to have been torpedoed by a German submarine.*

49

ships" if they remained outside the three-mile limit, but it chased, seized, and searched the American contact boats, which were called rumrunners. This was an enormous task. Many of the rumrunners were new and fast, so the Coast Guard had to buy and equip many new boats in order to keep up with the smugglers; it also began to patrol with airplanes. Because the profitable trade lured large numbers of adventurers, the Coast Guard also had to recruit and train another 5,000 men. It seemed that no sooner had one rumrunner been shut down than another two sprang up to take its place.

The "Rum War at Sea," as it was called, claimed some casualties. In a famous case, a coastguardsman was killed after boarding a Florida boat that was carrying 20 cases of whiskey; the smuggler responsible was hanged at the Coast Guard base in Fort Lauderdale. The battle between rumrunners and the Coast Guard took many forms. The rumrunners often resorted to tricks such as faking distress signals to get Coast Guard cutters out of the way so that they could make their shipments in safety (under Coast Guard policy, a distress signal always takes priority over other actions). Rumrunners sometimes dumped their cargoes when cutters approached; later they would raise the liquor, which had been attached to submerged buoys. Ironically, the rumrunners and mother ships, known to carry large sums of cash and liquor, became the targets of modern-day offshore pirates and sometimes had to seek the protection of the Coast Guard when they were attacked. One of the most unpleasant aspects of the situation for the guardsmen was the way they were treated by the public. Many people disapproved of Prohibition, and—as in the days of Jefferson's embargo—the Coast Guard became the target of much resentment and criticism. In several large cities, coastguardsmen were even harassed by angry mobs.

But the "Rum War" dragged on, and the Coast Guard achieved some victories. Its biggest single catch was the *Holewood*. Painted to resemble a well-known boat called the *Texas Ranger*, the *Holewood* tried to sail into New York with half a million dollars' worth of contraband alcohol. However, an alert Coast Guard officer posted at the mouth of New York harbor remembered a dispatch he had seen the previous day that stated the *Texas Ranger*'s location as the Gulf of Mexico. Suspicious, he allowed the ship to pass; he then called ahead to alert armed Coast Guard patrol boats, which greeted the *Holewood* as it entered the harbor.

Finally, in 1933, a new amendment repealed Prohibition. Liquor was now legal again, so smuggling became less profitable. It did not end entirely, however. Liquor and cigarettes continued to be smuggled into the country

A "mother ship" waits with cases of rum on deck for rapid transfer to smaller ships that will bring the illicit liquor ashore. During Prohibition, the Coast Guard was called upon to fight such smuggling.

throughout the 1930s and 1940s to evade taxes. Also during those years, smugglers began to trade American guns for Central American narcotics. Since the end of the Rum War, the Coast Guard has been part of the battle against drug smuggling.

World War II brought the Coast Guard under the Navy Department again, from 1941 to 1945. The service had three major duties during the war. One was the Greenland patrol, a weather and military patrolling service around Greenland and the North Atlantic. A surprising amount of action took place in the frozen north; the cutters *Eastwind* and *Northland* captured German spies and radio stations in Greenland.

Another duty was coast patrol offshore and along U.S. beaches. Coast patrollers watched for enemy submarines, rescued more than 2,500 victims of torpedo attacks, and monitored harbors, docks, and beaches for signs of espionage or sabotage. Many of the coast patrollers were trained civilian volunteers. At sea, they manned sailing craft, including some yachts donated by their owners. Ashore, they rode horses to cover more territory and save fuel. About 11,000 women volunteers took over many of the Coast Guard's onshore duties during the war.

The third wartime duty of the service drew upon its skill and experience in brown-water navigation and combat. Coast Guard vessels carried Allied troops through the surf to the beaches of Normandy, France, and landed U.S. Marines on the coral island of Guam, in the Pacific. The Coast Guard was involved in every sea-to-land invasion in France, Italy, North Africa, and the Pacific. Guardsmen manned 802 of their own cutters, 351 navy ships and boats, and 288 army vessels. A total of 1,917 coastguardsmen were lost during the war.

American soldiers disembark from Coast Guard landing barges to storm the beach at Normandy, France, on June 6, 1944. During World War II, the Guard came under the jurisdiction of the U.S. Navy, which frequently called upon its skill and experience in brown-water navigation.

Like the other services, the Coast Guard returned to peacetime status in 1946. In the decades since then, however, it has been called upon to lend support in two more wars. During the Korean War, 12 cutters operated weather stations, maintained port security, and guarded airfields in the Pacific. The Coast Guard's brown-water skills were especially valuable during the Vietnam War; a total of 56 cutters served in the muddy waters of Vietnam's canals and rivers, in the Mekong Delta, and off the coasts of Southeast Asia. They were charged with preventing enemies from getting into South Vietnam by sea and with the safe handling of ammunition and explosives. Coast Guard pilots also flew in the Rescue and Recovery Squadron, helping to rescue stranded soldiers and sailors from hostile territory.

Although maintaining a state of readiness for military action is one of its three main missions, the Coast Guard has not been called upon to perform military duties since the Vietnam War. But its peacetime duties, in the two broad areas of law enforcement and safety at sea, are still growing.

A Coast Guard official arrests a drug smuggler. The Coast Guard works with other law-enforcement agencies but often finds itself in the forefront of showdowns with smugglers because most drugs enter the United States by water.

FOUR

Police of the Waterways

About half of the Coast Guard's day-to-day activities can be considered law enforcement, which includes making sure that ships of all nations obey U.S. laws governing navigation and shipping while in U.S. waters and that U.S. ships obey these laws wherever they are. Beyond this, the service is responsible for enforcing, or helping other agencies to enforce, all federal laws—on the nation's waterways, in ports and coastal waters, and in international waters when appropriate. This responsibility is broad, yet in practice most of the Coast Guard's maritime law-enforcement duties fall into five programs: inspection and licensing; recreational boating; port safety and security; international treaties and conservation laws; and the war on smuggling.

Inspection and Licensing

The Coast Guard's marine inspection and licensing functions are aimed primarily at the merchant marine, the nation's commercial shipping fleet. Although these functions—the modern descendants of the old Steamboat Inspection Service—involve the enforcement of laws and regulations, they are also considered an important part of the service's mission to ensure safety at

The Coast Guard supervises the construction and operation of commercial ships at every stage. Inspection and licensing of these ships is one of the Guard's most crucial duties.

sea, because their purpose is to make sure that commercial vessels are safe and seaworthy and that their crews and officers are properly trained.

The Coast Guard supervises the construction and operation of commercial ships at every stage, from the drawing board to the scrap heap. The service regularly inspects American ships to ensure that they conform to safety regulations—they should have, for example, the necessary number of lifeboats, life preservers, and fire extinguishers. It also inspects foreign ships that carry passengers from American ports. In addition, the Coast Guard investigates collisions, fires, or other accidents on the water, both to determine who was responsible and to try to prevent future accidents.

Recreational Boating

Pleasure boating is big business in the United States. More than 16 million boats now carry more than 50 million boaters over the nation's lakes, rivers, and coastal waters. Although federal legislation gives the Coast Guard the right to inspect any craft for safety, the service is not often directly involved with the average recreational boater. Instead, the Coast Guard works behind the scenes with the designers and manufacturers of recreational boats to make sure that the craft are as safe as they can be.

Alcohol abuse and boating are a potentially deadly combination. The Coast Guard offers aid to states and boater-education organizations to promote awareness of the dangers of drinking alcohol.

A Coast Guard official teaches knot tying in a Guard-sponsored boating-safety class. Nearly half a million recreational boaters each year take such a course.

In the 1970s, with recreational boating growing at a record rate, the Coast Guard launched a national campaign to make boaters more aware of safety rules and safe boating habits; in fact, boater safety was one of the service's major areas of emphasis in that decade. Since that time, the Coast Guard has phased itself out of the day-to-day administration of recreational boating, which is largely the responsibility of the individual states. Although the Coast Guard recommends uniform boating-safety regulations, these rules—and the degree to which they are enforced—differ somewhat from state to state. The Guard also provides states and boater-education organizations with posters and educational materials to discourage alcohol use on the water.

Currently, recreational boaters are not required to attend boating-safety classes. Nonetheless, nearly half a million of them do so each year. Most such classes are taught by volunteers who have been trained by the Coast Guard.

Port Safety and Security

Almost 1,200 members of the Coast Guard are assigned to safety-and-security jobs in 47 ports. The captain of the port in each location is responsible for ensuring three things: the safety of people and property in the port and the surrounding shoreside area; the security of the port from sabotage, espionage, and crime; and the protection of the port environment from pollution and abuse.

Port safety-and-security teams oversee the handling of hazardous or explosive cargoes. They can order the removal of vessels that seem unsafe or that are carrying improperly secured cargoes. They carry out regular harbor patrols and, if a vessel or waterfront building seems suspicious, they can search it. One aspect of national security that is routinely handled by the Coast Guard is keeping track of all vessels from Communist-bloc nations that enter U.S. waters or ports.

A Coast Guard port-patrol crew. The Coast Guard is responsible for protecting people and property from crime and pollution in 47 ports across the country.

International Treaties
and Conservation Laws

The Coast Guard is responsible for seeing that international maritime treaties and agreements are obeyed in U.S. waters. Such agreements cover many subjects, from waste dumping to nuclear testing. In practice, though, most of the Coast Guard's work in this area is concerned with enforcing international fishing-rights agreements and conservation laws.

Conservation enforcement by the service has a long history. In 1822, Congress established protected forests of timber for use in the national fleet and assigned the Revenue Marine cutters to patrol for illegal logging along the coasts of these forests. Later in that century, the acquisition of Alaska brought new conservation needs. Fur seals gather in immense numbers on Alaska's Pribilof Islands to breed. Valued for their pelts, the seals were slaughtered at a rate of 75,000 a year during the first 4 years of U.S. control. In 1870, Congress began limiting the number that could be killed. Starting in 1894, bands of revenue mariners camped on the islands during breeding season to prevent poaching. In 1908, the Revenue Cutter Service was authorized to

Fur seals line an Alaska beach. The Coast Guard has historically protected such animals from poachers.

In 1972, the Coast Guard cutter Storis *confiscated the* Lamut, *a Soviet fishing vessel, after it discovered the Soviet ship fishing in U.S. territorial waters.*

enforce all of Alaska's fish and game laws. Around the same time, the service was charged with enforcing limits on fish catches in other U.S. waters and on the harvest of sponges in the Gulf of Mexico.

In 1976, Congress passed the Fishery Conservation and Management Act, which created a protected fishing zone under U.S. control that extends 200 miles off U.S. coasts. Now that the food resources of the ocean are of growing interest to a hungry world, commercial fishing is becoming more competitive, mechanized, and far-ranging. The Coast Guard cooperates with the U.S. Fish and Wildlife Service to protect fish and crustacean resources within the Fishery Conservation Zone—especially halibut, salmon, cod, and several kinds of crab—from foreign poachers. Cutters patrol the enormous zone, and their crews levy fines on illegal fishing boats. On occasion such boats have been confiscated. In January 1972, the Coast Guard cutter *Storis* seized the *Lamut*, a Soviet factory-fishing ship, and two other Russian vessels for fishing inside the U.S. territorial limit, which was then 12 miles offshore. The 3 skippers were fined a total of $250,000—the largest fine that had ever been assessed by the United States for infringement of fishing regulations.

The War on Smuggling

On the morning of February 19, 1988, the Coast Guard cutter *Mallow* and the navy vessel *Ouellet*, both based in Hawaii, began following a 160-foot Panamanian cruiser named *Christina M* as it steamed northward about 800 miles southeast of Hawaii. Members of a special multiagency team to fight drug traffic had reason to believe that the *Christina M* might be a drug smuggler. The 2 vessels kept the cruiser in sight for almost 24 hours until they received permission from the government of Panama to board it.

The captain of the *Christina M* was not happy about being boarded, but the skipper of the *Mallow* assured him that the Coast Guard had not only the right but also the muscle to do so. An hour later, searchers in one of the cruiser's cargo holds discovered 454 bales of marijuana, each weighing 55 pounds. The boarding party arrested 8 of the *Christina M*'s crew, transferred them to the *Mallow*, and started steaming toward Honolulu with the prisoners—and $12 million worth of contraband drugs.

Four days later, as the rock song "Smuggler's Blues" blared mockingly from its loudspeakers, the *Mallow* arrived at its dock and was greeted by a crowd of reporters and newscasters. It was the largest drug bust in Hawaii's history and the second largest ever made in the Pacific. But the arrests did not end there. The *Christina M* was a mother ship and had already unloaded some of its illegal cargo to smaller vessels bound for the West Coast. A few days later, 2 of them were intercepted in California and 12 more smugglers were arrested.

The case of the *Christina M* is a shining success story in the area that has become the most visible of the Coast Guard's activities in the 1980s: drug interdiction, or the enforcing of laws against illegal drugs. In a new sort of Prohibition Era, the Coast Guard—along with other federal and law-enforcement agencies—has taken up arms in the battle against drugs. The *Christina M* case illustrates the teamwork among agencies that is the hallmark of today's antidrug crusade. The seizure of the cruiser and its crew was a joint effort by the navy, the State Department (which conducted talks with the Panamanian government), the Customs Department (which took custody of the drug ship), the National Narcotics Border Interdiction System (a system of coordination between federal, state, and local law-enforcement agencies with

Coast Guard officials chase a suspected drug smuggler off the Florida coast. Helicopters play a vital role in Coast Guard operations, especially SAR missions.

overlapping jurisdictions), and local law-enforcement officials, as well as the Coast Guard. But, although it relies on help from other agencies, the Guard often finds itself in the forefront of showdowns with smugglers, because most drugs enter the United States by water.

The drug war is particularly hot in the waters off Florida, where smugglers ceaselessly run drugs up from South America. The Coast Guard's patrol of the Miami area is one of the most intensive anywhere. It concentrates on three key lines of defense. The first line is at the "choke points," narrow straits or passages between islands in the Caribbean through which the larger drug ships—the mother ships—must pass on their way north. The Guard sends its largest cutters, the 210- and 378-footers, to patrol these choke points for 3 or 4 weeks at a stretch. The second line is about 200 miles off the Florida coast, the point at which those mother ships that make it through the choke points usually offload their cargoes onto smaller vessels for the run to shore; the Guard stations 95- and 110-foot cutters along this line. At the third line of defense, smaller Coast Guard craft, from 18 to 41 feet in length, operate from shore stations and try to catch the fast drug boats coming in.

A Coast Guard crew offers aid to Cuban refugees off the Florida coast in 1980. Although illegal immigration poses a dilemma for U.S. lawmakers, the Coast Guard must uphold the law and return such would-be immigrants to their homeland.

In the late 1980s, the Coast Guard seized an average of about 200 drug boats and 2.5 million pounds of illegal drugs each year, resulting in some 800 arrests annually. But the profits to be made in the drug trade are alluring, and the smugglers are tireless, numerous, and often equipped with boats and weapons as good as—or better than—those of the law enforcers. Coast Guard officials admit that for every drug boat they stop, two or three slip through, simply because there are not enough people and boats to catch them all.

Different in many ways from the high-tech world of big-time drug smuggling is another kind of smuggling that occurs in the same waters: the traffic in illegal immigrants. Cutter crews often spot small boats, usually overcrowded and unsafe, filled with people from Caribbean islands or Central or South America who have paid the captains to smuggle them into the United States—without going through the formalities required by the U.S. Immigration and Naturalization Service. Several thousand such would-be immigrants are returned to their points of origin each year. Some of the illegal immigrants have been rescued after their vessels capsized or sprang a leak or after they ran out of food or water. Not everyone in the United States believes that these "boat people" should be forced to return to their homes; some view them as refugees, rather than illegal aliens, and feel that they should be allowed to enter the country. But, although the issue is controversial, the Coast Guard continues to uphold the current law of the land, just as Alexander Hamilton intended it to do.

Guardsmen from the Pacific-based ocean station Pontchartrain *race to the scene of the 1956 Pan American clipper plane crash. As airline safety improved over the next two decades, ocean stations were no longer needed.*

FIVE

Safety at Sea

Side by side with its law-enforcement activities, the Coast Guard carries out a variety of programs aimed at safeguarding lives and property at sea. In recent years, the concept of safety at sea has been broadened to include the safety of the marine environment as well, and the Guard has an important responsibility in environmental protection. As with the drug-interdiction program and other law-enforcement activities, the men and women of the Guard often work with people from other agencies and services to carry out certain parts of their safety-at-sea mission.

Search and Rescue

Of all the Coast Guard's safety activities, probably the best known is Search and Rescue, or SAR, as it is called within the service. Since the days of Joshua James and Sumner Kimball, lifesaving has called forth the best efforts of shore teams and cutter crews in the rescue of lives in peril at sea. Today, rescue operations take priority over all other peacetime duties of the Coast Guard. Cutters and patrol boats on duty in fishing waters, drug choke points, or harbors will unfailingly interrupt their scheduled operations to respond to a distress call.

The Coast Guard rescues flood victims in Tennessee in the 1930s.

SAR practices have changed over the years, reflecting changes in technology and in the way people use the sea. In the early days, most efforts were concentrated on rescuing people from wrecks along the nation's shores; the rocket-launched line (a lifeline fired by a cannon or artillery gun), the oared lifeboat, and the surf car formed the lifesavers' arsenal. During this era, from 1830 to about 1870, ships carrying immigrants were the most frequent coastal wrecks. Later, steel construction and steam power made possible larger cargo and passenger vessels, and this development, combined with better navigational equipment, caused shipping to shift into the open sea-lanes.

New rescue equipment and techniques developed to meet the needs of large-volume, high-seas traffic. The "blue-water" cutter, designed for duty far from land, became important in rescue work at the turn of the century. Shortly thereafter, the development of radio made it possible for ships to communicate with one another and with the shore—suddenly, ships at sea out of sight of land could broadcast distress calls. By 1915, all the Coast Guard's cruising cutters had radios. In the 1930s, seaplanes began to be used in rescue operations. When regular passenger airline service across the Atlantic began just before World War II, plane crashes at sea brought about a new lifesaving operation: the ocean station. An ocean station was a large cutter positioned permanently in midocean to serve as a base for rescue missions and also to issue weather reports to ships and planes. Ocean stations were set up in the Atlantic and Pacific oceans and the Gulf of Mexico. They proved their usefulness in such cases as that of the Pan American clipper plane that went down in the Pacific in October 1956; the crew of the ocean station cutter *Pontchartrain* managed to rescue all 31 people aboard. By the 1970s, however, aircraft safety had improved, and the ocean stations were no longer vital to the service's lifesaving efforts. They were phased out by 1977.

SAR includes not only saving lives at sea but also helping the victims of floods on shore. When rains or hurricanes cause flooding, the Coast Guard rushes emergency equipment to the scene. In the 1920s and 1930s, lifeboats from the East Coast were sent by train to help victims of floods in the Tennessee Valley. In 1965, 11 Coast Guard helicopters made 140 flights into areas flooded by Hurricane Betsy along the coast of Louisiana; their crews

In 1979, Hurricane Frederick devastated areas in the South. The Coast Guard's SAR program provides emergency aid to victims of such natural disasters as hurricanes and floods.

rescued 1,144 people and carried 22 doctors to emergency calls. Today, one of the first sights one perceives when a river is rising, or a tropical storm is moving in, is the orange stripes on the Guard's white choppers.

The helicopter is a vital part of modern Coast Guard operations. During World War II, the government assigned to the Guard the task of adapting helicopters for antisubmarine warfare, and Coast Guard instructors trained all American and British helicopter pilots. After the war, the Coast Guard recognized the enormous usefulness of the helicopter in SAR missions. Rescuers can survey a wider range of sea from a chopper than from a ship, and they can get closer to the area than in an airplane. Additionally, unlike planes, helicopters can hover while they lower ropes or safety equipment to victims of shipwreck or fire. Helicopters were able to hoist crewmen to safety from the decks of the burning 500-foot Peruvian tanker *Inca Tupac Yupanqui* in 1979; without choppers, that rescue would have been much more difficult—perhaps impossible. In the 1970s and 1980s, the enormous growth of recreational

Helicopters are crucial to the modern Coast Guard's Search and Rescue program.

Buzzard's Bay light station was the first offshore fixed light tower to replace a lightship. By the late 20th century, lighted buoys and towers sunk into the ocean-bed had replaced older navigational technology such as lightships.

boating has shifted the scene of much of the SAR effort back toward coastal waters, and the shore-based helicopter is one of the Coast Guard's most important rescue tools.

Aids to Navigation

The Lighthouse Service, the oldest of the many organizations that combined to form the modern Coast Guard, is represented today by the Guard's Aids to Navigation program. An aid to navigation is anything that helps a mariner determine his precise position, set a safe course, and avoid obstructions or dangers.

Like the tools of SAR, the technology of navigation aids has changed a great deal over the years. In colonial times, lighthouses dotted the headlands of the East Coast; bells were rung when fog threatened to obscure their beams. Lightships came into use in 1820. More than 100 lightships existed by the early 20th century. Today, all but one have been replaced by large buoys or lights on deep-sunk pilings.

An OMEGA station tower. The OMEGA navigation system emits electronic beams that ships can pick up and use to precisely plot their positions.

Present aids to navigation fall into two broad groups. Short-range aids include offshore light platforms, lighthouses (now almost entirely automated, with battery-operated lights), fog signals, buoys, channel markers, and radar beacons. Most of these aids are located in U.S. inland waterways and coastal waters. Long-range aids include radio beacons and two systems of electronic broadcasting, LORAN-C and OMEGA.

LORAN-C, like radar, was developed during World War II. It emits a beam that can be picked up at very long range; a ship that can pick up signals from 3 LORAN-C stations can plot its position precisely—to within 1,000 feet—at a distance of more than 1,000 miles from the nearest station. The Coast Guard operates 28 LORAN-C stations in U.S. territory and another 10 in overseas locations, including the Arctic, the Middle East, the Western Pacific, and Europe.

The newest navigation technology is the OMEGA system. It is an electronic broadcasting system similar to LORAN-C, except that its wavelength can be received at much greater range, so that complete coverage of the globe can be achieved with fewer stations and less expense. The Guard maintains an OMEGA station in Hawaii and one in the continental United States; six other

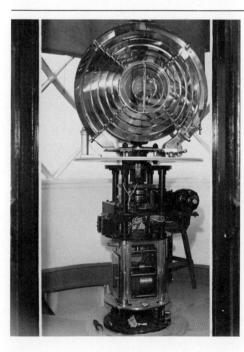

Inside a modern lighthouse. Since lighthouses came into widespread use in the 18th century, lighthouse technology has changed a great deal. Today, nearly all of the Coast Guard's lighthouses are fully automated and visited only by maintenance crews.

stations around the world are jointly paid for by the United States and allied nations and are administered by the Coast Guard.

Governor's Island, in New York harbor, is the site of the Guard's Aids to Navigation School, where new technology—such as special plastics for lighthouse lenses that throw more light farther with less power—is adapted to navigational use. There Coast Guard men and women are trained in the use, maintenance, and repair of the aids. The Guard base in New York also contains a sophisticated computer that can keep track of up to 2,300 commercial ships anywhere in the world. Using constantly updated information about winds and tides, the computer can also pinpoint the most likely places to look for drifting ships, lifeboats, or rafts. In a typical example of how the different programs within the Coast Guard cooperate, this computer is both an aid to navigation and a powerful SAR tool. The Coast Guard uses it and other tools to coordinate rescue efforts around the world, even in places that are out of reach of Guard cutters; many rescues on the high seas are truly international ventures, with government and commercial vessels from many nations pitching in.

Bridge Administration

When it became part of the Department of Transportation in 1967, the Coast Guard acquired responsibility for administering the construction, maintenance, and operation of all bridges across navigable U.S. waterways—that is, across rivers, bays, canals, and channels that have boat traffic. Although the Coast Guard does not carry out all of these activities directly, it is responsible for coordinating the work of local, state, and other federal agencies concerning bridges.

Vessel Traffic Services

Closely related to the Aids to Navigation program is Vessel Traffic Services, which operates high-technology traffic-control centers in six of the nation's busiest ports. This program was begun after two tankers crashed into one another in the fog in San Francisco harbor in 1971. It is now used in San Francisco, New York, New Orleans, Houston, Seattle, and Valdez, Alaska—all ports with large-volume oceangoing traffic and long, narrow entrances that invite collision when they become crowded. Coast Guard members use radio,

A worker at the Coast Guard's Houston Vessel Traffic Services center uses closed-circuit television to monitor ships and help them avoid collisions in the busy port.

radar, and closed-circuit television to monitor the movements of oceangoing vessels as they enter or leave port; ship symbols on a large harbor map show the positions of all ships at all times.

Ice Operations

The Coast Guard's responsibilities regarding ice go back to the 1890s, the days of the Bering Sea Patrol, when revenue mariners in Alaskan waters learned to go around or—if necessary—through ice to do their jobs. This practice took a step forward with the formation of the International Ice Patrol (IIP) after the 1912 *Titanic* disaster. Today, the Ice Operations program covers two areas of activity: the IIP and icebreaking.

The IIP does its work in the North Atlantic, near the Grand Banks of Newfoundland—dangerous seas, but also rich in fish and located on the most fuel-efficient shipping route between Europe and North America. The danger in these waters comes from the enormous ice-covered island of Greenland, far to the north. In the spring, massive chunks of ice break free of the Greenland ice pack and are carried south on the Labrador current, where they drift into fishing grounds and shipping lanes. At the same place, worsening the situation, the cold Labrador current meets the warm Gulf Stream, and the temperature difference between the two water masses produces dense banks of fog for almost half of each year. Severe storms and fixed-location oil-drilling platforms add to the potential for trouble. The IIP helps reduce that potential by locating icebergs and reporting their position, enabling mariners to avoid these floating hazards. On occasion, especially threatening bergs have been exploded or even towed out of the way.

The Coast Guard has patrolled the region during the ice season—March through September—every year since 1914, except for a few years during the world wars. Cutters were used for the patrol until 1980, but the job is now done from airplanes equipped with special airborne radar devices. However, cutters are still stationed in the iceberg zone for rescue, research, and supplemental patrolling. The results of IIP survey flights, along with reports of iceberg sightings from commercial ships and airplanes, are broadcast to IIP headquarters in Groton, Connecticut, and plotted on a computer. Transmitters at Groton broadcast bulletins twice daily; these broadcasts are then relayed by the U.S. Navy and Canadian and European stations. The IIP also makes a scientific contribution. It carries out ocean science research on the composition, sources, and drift patterns of icebergs and on how currents are shaped by wind and the structure of the seafloor. Data from drifting buoys and radio beacons located on icebergs, used to track the bergs, is also added to scientific records kept by the National Oceanographic and Atmospheric Administration.

The second area of the Guard's Ice Operations program is icebreaking. The Guard has four large ships called icebreakers that can force a passage through ice by driving their immensely strong reinforced-steel bows into the ice; the weight of the ship and the pressure of its engines driving forward then crush or split the ice. Two of the ships are stationed on the Great Lakes to break open frozen shipping lanes for ore carriers and other commercial vessels. The other two are equipped for polar expeditions to the Arctic Sea or Antarctica; they carry scientists from a variety of government and academic organizations to isolated bases where research is being conducted on such subjects as Arctic weather patterns and the damaged ozone layer (a shield of atmospheric gases that protects the earth from solar radiation) over Antarctica. In addition to providing supply transport to these expeditions, the ships also support military and defense operations in the polar regions by breaking channels for navy

The Coast Guard's Ice Operations program covers two areas of activity: the International Ice Patrol (IIP), which sometimes goes as far as exploding icebergs (top) to ensure safe passage for ships through the region, and icebreaking (bottom).

ships. The Coast Guard is the only federal agency that operates icebreakers and is therefore involved in all polar activities. It also maintains about nine smaller tugboats reinforced for breaking the thinner ice of inland and coastal U.S. waterways.

Environmental Response

Like lifesaving and navigation aids, the Environmental Response program is the modern descendant of duties that were carried out by the Coast Guard's predecessors. In 1899, Congress passed the Refuse Act, one of the nation's first antipollution laws. It was enforced jointly by the Army Corps of Engineers and the Revenue Cutter Service.

Since then, both the problems of pollution and the number of protective regulations have increased tremendously. Under the Federal Water Pollution Control Act of 1976, the Coast Guard—along with many other agencies and services—tries to minimize pollution in the marine environment. The Coast Guard's role is chiefly to take whatever safety and protective measures are possible when a pollutant or hazardous material is detected in the water. The Port Safety and Security program prevents or controls small oil or chemical spills in the nation's harbors; in a crisis situation, safety-and-security personnel will call in an environmental response team.

A pelican at a makeshift bird sanctuary at the Coast Guard's San Juan, Puerto Rico, base. The Guard cleaned and fed the more than 500 pelicans that were injured in 1968 when the tanker Ocean Eagle *ran aground and spilled its cargo of 2 million gallons of oil.*

When the Argo Merchant *ran aground off the Massachusetts coast in 1976, the Coast Guard's Environmental Response Strike Force supervised cleanup of the more than 7 million gallons of oil that spilled from the disabled craft.*

Throughout its history, the Coast Guard has added or acquired new responsibilities whenever new problems or conditions demanded them. One of the most recent problems to arise at sea has been oil pollution. The number of large-scale spills from tankers, pipelines, and oil rigs increased drastically in the late 1960s and early 1970s. In 1968, the tanker *Ocean Eagle* ran aground near San Juan, Puerto Rico, and broke in half, spilling more than 2 million gallons of oil. The Coast Guard unit in San Juan responded by towing the tanker away, monitoring the oil spill, and—in a spirit of environmental protection—turning its base into a bird sanctuary for cleaning and feeding more than 500 pelicans that had been soaked with oil.

In 1973, the Guard formed a special strike force to respond immediately when oil is spilled. It uses the most advanced technology available, including rubber tanks that can be dropped from planes to transfer oil from disabled tankers and systems of floating barriers to keep oil from washing ashore. The strike force's first major challenge was a spill from the *Metula* off the tip of South America in 1974. The *Argo Merchant* ran aground off Massachusetts in 1976, spilling 7.3 million gallons; the Coast Guard Strike Force supervised cleanup operations. As more offshore drilling rigs are built and tankers and supertankers ply the seas in increasing numbers to satisfy the world's hunger for fuel, it is likely that the need for prevention, control, and cleanup of spills will continue.

79

Hamilton Hall, the administration building at the Coast Guard Academy in New London, Connecticut, is named for the Coast Guard's creator, Alexander Hamilton.

SIX

Inside the Coast Guard

T he Coast Guard's military structure and ranks are parallel to those of the navy. The head of the Guard always holds the rank of admiral; while directing the Guard, he is given the title of commandant. His headquarters is in Washington, D.C., as is that of the Guard's parent organization, the Department of Transportation. Unlike purely desk-bound organizations, however, the Coast Guard has a decentralized administration—in other words, leadership is spread out to cover the area in which the Guard's real work is done.

The next level below the commandant is area commander. The two area commanders have the rank of vice admiral. The commander of the Pacific area is based in Alameda, California. He is responsible for Coast Guard operations in Alaska, Hawaii, and the eight westernmost states of the continental United States, as well as the entire Pacific Ocean region. The commander of the Atlantic area is based on Governor's Island, New York, and is responsible for the East Coast, Great Lakes, Gulf Coast, Midwest, and Great Plains states. His responsibility extends to Coast Guard operations throughout the Atlantic Ocean. Each area also has a commander with the rank of rear admiral who is responsible for the necessary maintenance, purchasing, and other support programs throughout the area.

Boot Camp

The military career of each newly enlisted recruit in the U.S. armed forces starts with a short, grueling season of toughening up, weeding out, and whipping into shape. This physical and mental initiation is called *boot camp*. The Coast Guard's boot camp is its Recruit Training Center at Cape May, New Jersey, where some 5,000 young men and women each year complete an 8-and-a-half-week program that prepares them for field duty.

Tucked away in a popular seaside resort, Station Cape May looks, at first glance, like a vacation camp: tennis courts, a softball field, powerboats tied up at the docks—a great place to spend a couple of months. But near the tennis courts are classroom buildings where recruits spend many hours learning—and being tested on—such subjects as military courtesy, Coast Guard history, and the correct way to wear a uniform. The station has other features not common in resorts, such as the indoor rifle range, where recruits learn to handle and fire .9 mm pistols and M16 machine guns, and the fire simulator, a small, charred building that instructors set on fire to test the recruits' mastery of their fire-fighting lessons.

The obstacle course, with nets to climb and walls to scale, suggests that fitness is serious business at this camp. One of the first tests facing each recruit is in the large gym, where he or she must do push-ups, sit-ups, and other exercises under the critical eye of an instructor. On this first day, most of the recruits are unable to complete the required number of repetitions. After breaking into a sweat in the gym, they move down the hall to the Olympic-sized pool for the first in a series of training sessions in swimming, lifesaving, and drownproofing. Surprisingly, many recruits join the Coast Guard without knowing how to swim. They learn. And when they graduate from boot camp, they are in the best shape of their life and equipped with a lifetime fitness program.

Recruits on the obstacle course.

Recruits practice the line handling skill necessary to dock a large ship.

The deck seamanship area is a large, open square, a stone's throw from the docks. Here, where the ground sprouts cleats (two-pronged fittings around which a rope may be fastened), bollards (posts for fastening mooring lines), and features usually found only on the decks of ships, fourth-week recruits learn the fundamentals of handling and knotting lines, taking the helm, and holding a steady course—all on dry land. The recruits also spend time aboard a vessel such as the 210-foot cutter *Alert,* one of more than half a dozen ships stationed at Cape May.

Although practices and procedures at the Coast Guard's Recruit Training Center have mellowed in recent years, Coast Guard recruits remain under intense pressure. The fundamental purpose of boot camp is to weed out recruits who cannot take such pressure *before* they are faced with a real life-and-death situation. More than one-fifth of those who enter the program do not finish it; these recruits drop out for medical or psychological reasons or because the Coast Guard decides that they are not fit for service. But those who have guts, intelligence, and the right attitude usually survive. After perhaps the longest eight weeks of their life, they are ready for their first duty assignments— and for the next four years in the Coast Guard.

U.S. Coast Guard Areas

U.S. Coast Guard areas of command. The Guard divides the country into a Pacific area and an Atlantic area; these regions are further subdivided into a total of 10 districts.

The 2 areas are subdivided into a total of 10 districts—4 in the Pacific area and 6 in the Atlantic area. Each district is headed by a district commander who has the rank of rear admiral and reports to the area commander. Each district commander is responsible for all activities in his district, except for cutters exceeding 100 feet in length; the captains of these boats report directly to the area commanders.

Smaller stations within each district may report directly to the district commander; in some districts, however, several stations report to a group commander, who in turn reports to the district commander. The Guard maintains a total of 1,234 shore stations, ranging from LORAN-C bases on Pacific islets to 158 small-boat stations that concentrate on search-and-rescue operations.

The People of the Coast Guard

The size of the Coast Guard has remained fairly constant since 1972. In 1988, the Guard had a total of 37,959 people on active duty; 4,977 of them were officers. About 2,600 of them were women. The Coast Guard was the first of

One of the first enlisted women assigned to duty as a crew member on a coastal patrol of the United States, aboard the Coast Guard cutter Gallatin in 1978. The Coast Guard was the first of the armed forces to include women in its officer ranks.

the U.S. armed forces to open the doors of its officer academy to women and the first to give them command of armed vessels. Nearly 200 women held officer rank in 1988, and another 100 or so were expected to graduate from the officer academy by 1990.

Enlisted men and women enter the Coast Guard through the recruiting process; the Guard maintains recruiting offices in large cities, and potential recruits from other parts of the country can get information from the office of the commandant, in Washington, D.C. Once enlisted, they start their four-year tour of duty at the Cape May, New Jersey, station, with an eight-week course of basic training. Basic is tough; about 100 recruits start the program each week, and nearly 22 percent of them do not finish. Those who do are assigned to duty stations for on-the-job training. Many go on to receive advanced training in aviation, electronics, and other fields through graduate courses at universities, attendance at other services' academies, or correspondence courses from the Coast Guard Institute. Those who decide to stay in the Coast

The Eagle *is used as a training vessel for cadets at the Coast Guard Academy in New London.*

Troops at Officer Candidate School in Yorktown, Virginia. Although most Coast Guard officers are trained at the Coast Guard Academy, enlisted men and women can also become officers through training at OCS.

Guard and make it their career may enter a number of specialized professions, ranging from communications to environmental protection to financial management to law enforcement. Nearly all Coast Guard careers involve a number of years of sea duty.

Officers enter the Coast Guard from several sources. The Coast Guard Academy, located in New London, Connecticut, was founded in 1876 to train officers for the service. It is open to unmarried men and women between the ages of 17 and 22 who compete for openings in a system of nationwide examinations; admission is based strictly on merit. Once admitted, they follow a four-year course of study that includes typical college fare—history, chemistry, English—in addition to seamanship, military tactics, gunnery, radio, engineering, navigation, and other nonacademic subjects. Upon graduation, they receive bachelor of science degrees and are commissioned as ensigns— the bottom rung on the officers' ladder. They are required to complete a 5-year tour of duty; about 60 percent of them take additional graduate courses during that time. Overall, nearly 90 percent of the academy graduates remain with the Coast Guard after the 5 years are over. Although most of the Guard's officers come from the academy, enlisted men and women in regular Coast Guard

Swabs and Ensigns

It stinks the first year, it really stinks, but I just keep thinking that it's got to get better," says Amy Colleen Koepp. She is 18 years old and a cadet 4th class—the equivalent of a college freshman—at the Coast Guard Academy in New London, Connecticut. If Koepp makes it through the academy's four-year program, she will graduate with a bachelor of science degree in one of seven majors and a commission as ensign, the service's lowest-ranking officer, in the Coast Guard.

But for now Koepp is a "swab," as first-year cadets are called, and a swab's life is nothing like the pizza-and-late-nights romp that many students expect from their first year of college. It starts with "Swab Summer," six weeks that combine the worst features of boot camp, final exams, and the Iron Man Triathlon. "It's a big madhouse," Koepp says. "You have sports, lectures, tests. . . . You have to learn about service etiquette, you have to do everything just right. You never forget that you're in the military. It's like college with everything else piled on."

In addition to compulsory sports, such as survival swimming and gymnastics, Koepp takes five classes: chemistry, calculus, English, communications engineering and design, and coastal navigation. She is also in the drum and bugle corps and the glee club. "It's more difficult to fit everything in with those activities," she admits, "but they're the only way to meet people outside your class."

Koepp was attracted to the Coast Guard because it was different from the other services. "This one is more of a humanitarian service," she explains. "It's helping people all year round, not just preparation for war." She also likes the size of the academy—usually 750 to 900 cadets. "There's something about this place, being a small school—it doesn't force you, but it guides you to form strong bonds."

Women have been admitted to the academy since 1976, but they are still a miniority (about 17 percent in 1988). "Basically, when you're a woman here, it's one extreme or the other," says Koepp. "Either you slack off a little and everyone looks down on you, or you do what we call 'sucking it up.' That means doing the best you can, trying a little harder, and not letting anybody hear you whine." Koepp admits that some of the male cadets give the women a hard time, but she adds, "This summer, in my platoon, we didn't have a lot of problems. Everyone pulled together. That was a very positive experience."

Koepp faces a lot of hard work before she can have a chance to realize her dream of serving on an icebreaker. "They do push you hard here," she says, "and it's not what you could call fun, but look what you're getting—a really good education that's all paid for, a job when you get out . . . a future."

Another cadet who has done some thinking about the future is Andrew Liess, a 1st-classman, or senior, who is scheduled to graduate at age 22 in the spring of 1989. He has also encountered a few surprises. "I'm from a small town in Nebraska, and I'd never seen the ocean before reporting here as a 4th-classman," he recalls. "That summer, I had a one-week training cruise, and that was when I first realized what I was involved with. I was in awe of the sea. Now I spend every summer on the sea—last summer I sailed to Europe—and it's never old hat, but now I take it in stride."

Liess's feelings about the service have changed also. "Originially I came here thinking it would be a stepping-stone to the rest of my life, maybe in the business world, because it's a good education and the service academies have a certain prestige," he says. "Now I look at it differently. I see myself getting some shiphandling experience, maybe getting command of my own small patrol boat, and then, when my five years are up, maybe staying on for as long as the Coast Guard and I agree with each other."

He recalls two low spots in his own career as a cadet: "The first was Swab Summer; that's pretty disheartening. The second big down was realizing that *everyone* here was a top performer in high school, but now there's only going to be a few at the top."

A few months before graduation Liess's "Billet Night" will occur. The available duty postings will be listed on a blackboard, and the graduating cadets will choose postings in order of their class standing ("an impetus to do well," as Liess points out). If he gets his first choice, he will serve his first tour of duty on a 210-foot cutter in California or Florida, where he will be active in search-and-rescue and law-enforcement operations. And after that? "Maybe my own command, or perhaps a posting at headquarters in Washington while I go to night school for my master's in business administration," Liess says. "Looking back, there were times when I wondered what I was doing here, but I've grown to like it. I'm set up for a great future. How many guys my age can say that?"

service can become officers. They do not attend the academy; instead, if they qualify, they are trained at the Officer Candidate School at Yorktown, Virginia.

Yorktown is also the site of the Reserve Training Center. Like the other armed forces, the Coast Guard maintains a reserve of men and women who receive special training so that they can supplement the Guard's active-duty forces in time of war, emergency, or national disaster. Reservists start off with a form of basic training; thereafter, they have weekend drills once each month and serve two-week stints of active duty once each year, performing SAR and other tasks alongside active-duty personnel. In 1988, the Coast Guard Reserve numbered 12,254.

The Coast Guard Auxiliary is another group that is closely associated with the active-duty service. Auxiliarists are civilians who volunteer their time and skills to help the Coast Guard carry out its missions. Most of them are boaters; many own their own boats. Others are radio operators or pilots of private planes. They provide backup for the Guard in three key areas. First, they

The Coast Guard's Reserve Training Center in Yorktown, Virginia. The Coast Guard maintains a reserve of men and women who are trained to supplement active-duty forces in times of emergency, war, or national disaster.

Admiral Paul A. Yost, Jr., formerly the commander of the Coast Guard's Atlantic area, became the Guard's 18th commandant in 1986.

conduct most of the recreational boating-safety classes in the country. Second, they contribute mightily to search-and-rescue operations. Third, they patrol regattas, races, and other marine events for the Coast Guard. Although they are supervised by the Guard, they receive no pay, and little government funding is allotted to promote their programs. The Coast Guard considers the auxiliary a powerful and inexpensive ally that adds 35,000 trained volunteers, 9,000 boats, 1,200 radio stations, and 165 planes to its educational and lifesaving capacity.

Another organization to which the service has reason to be grateful is the Coast Guard Foundation, a civilian group founded in 1969 to help raise funds to supplement federal funding for the academy. Fund-raising efforts by the foundation have given the academy a visitors' center, crew training center, academic and athletic projects, and a recreational lodge. The foundation is directing its efforts to the rest of the service. It regularly holds fund-raising dinners in New York and San Francisco to honor Coast Guard heroes.

A coastguardsman on port-patrol duty. The Coast Guard conducted more than 19,000 such routine patrols in 1987.

SEVEN

Ready for
Tomorrow

The impact of the Coast Guard on the United States and the world can be measured in as many ways as the Coast Guard has responsibilities. Some of the key facts and figures are these:

- Drug Interdiction: 36 million tons of drugs seized, 1,506 vessels seized, and 7,281 arrests made from 1973 to 1987; marijuana worth $12.5 billion and cocaine worth $480 million seized from 1982 to 1986.

- Search and Rescue: 5,778 lives saved, 131,537 people otherwise assisted, and $903.6 million worth of property protected in 55,986 SAR responses during 1987; 707,000 people assisted and 30,700 lives saved from 1982 to 1986.

- Inspection and Licensing: 11,800 accidents investigated, 60,500 seamen's licenses issued, and 44,400 American and foreign vessels inspected in an average year.

- Aids to Navigation: 45,600 federal aids serviced and 42,000 private aids authorized in an average year.

- Environmental Response: 8,618 pollution reports received, 7,903 investigations conducted, 1,488 responsible-party cleanups, and 218 Coast Guard supervised cleanups in 1987.

Coast Guard officials inspect a boater's license. The Guard routinely stops pleasure boaters to check whether or not they are following safety regulations.

- Port Safety and Security: 6,826 cargo transfers monitored, 19,268 harbor patrols conducted, 4,799 safety examinations of foreign vessels carried out, and 5,295 waterfront facilities inspected in 1987.
- Treaty Enforcement: 26,801 aircraft-patrol hours and 11,335 cutter-patrol days logged, 2,414 fishing boats boarded, and $5.3 million in illegally caught fish seized in 1987.

The Coast Guard's total budget for 1988 was $2.5 billion. This was the lowest amount allocated to the service by the federal government in several years. Like many other federally funded agencies and services, the Coast Guard is facing the problem of whether to expand or even continue operations on a diminishing budget. The war on drugs, for example, is a top national priority, yet cutbacks and shortages in funding are keeping the Guard from doing more to combat smuggling; in particular, the Coast Guard commandant said in early 1988, more people, boats, and money are needed for the Guard to be as effective against cocaine as it has been against marijuana. Yet the Guard seized more than $3 billion worth of drugs in 1987—more than its entire annual budget.

Another area in which the service is feeling the pinch is Ice Operations. Some of its icebreakers are wearing out. The Guard will soon be down to two. It needs a new polar icebreaker, but these vessels are extremely costly, and Congress has been reluctant to authorize the expense. The Guard's marine-science research programs have become inactive in the late 1980s due to lack of funding, although many of them have been taken over by other agencies.

Another expensive area is Search and Rescue. Every response to a distress signal costs time, money, and fuel; quite often many boats and aircraft are involved in days-long searches. With drug interdiction getting greater emphasis in recent years—and therefore a bigger proportion of a shrinking budget—there has been less money for SAR. One solution that has been proposed is the user fee, which would require boaters and mariners to pay a part of the cost of the Coast Guard's services in aiding them. The concept of user fees is controversial, however, and is yet to become law; the Guard cannot count on it in planning its budget.

Wherever possible, the Guard looks for ways to make its dollars go further. Since 1982, it has converted more than 6,000 battery-powered navigation aids to solar power; this leads to fewer service visits and lower operating costs. The switch from manned to automated lighthouses has saved almost $22 million over the past 20 years.

First Lady Nancy Reagan inspects a display of drug paraphernalia during a 1982 drug-abuse conference at the White House. Although the Reagan administration pledged to fight an all-out battle against illegal drug trafficking—a battle fought off the nation's coasts by the U.S. Coast Guard—many critics charged that the administration's effort was lukewarm at best.

A Coast Guard official working with the Greenland Glacier Survey takes a water sample. The Guard is the main U.S. participant in the International Marine Organization, a group whose member countries pool their knowledge to increase international cooperation in areas such as pollution prevention, SAR, and fishing rights.

The history of the Coast Guard has been one of change and adaptation to new needs and new problems. In keeping with its motto, *Semper Paratus*—Always Ready—the Guard is trying to adapt to present needs and prepare for future challenges. The oil-pollution strike force is an example of a recent adaptation to meet a need. A current example is the development of new technology that will enable Coast Guard crews to use airplanes to search wide areas of the Gulf of Mexico and the Caribbean for drug-carrying planes; equipped with infrared and electronic sensors, these aircraft are also helpful in pinpointing disabled craft and floating survivors during SAR missions. One ongoing communications challenge is the promotion of voluntary safety in America's fishing fleet, which is not covered by commercial licensing regulations. The Coast Guard hopes to reduce casualties—and SAR missions—by making owners and operators of fishing vessels more safety conscious, and so far the effort seems to have achieved some success.

96

One tool that may help the Coast Guard stay ready for whatever comes along is the International Marine Organization (IMO), part of the United Nations. Numbering more than 100, the member countries of the IMO pool their knowledge in an effort to increase international cooperation in matters such as pollution prevention, SAR, and fishing rights. The Coast Guard is the center of U.S. participation in IMO projects.

Stopping smugglers and saving lives—two of the oldest missions of the Coast Guard—are its most visible peacetime activities today. It is likely that the Guard will continue to shift more resources toward drug interdiction in the 1990s, and, if budget needs are not met, some of its other programs may suffer as a result. But as long as drug interdiction is a national goal, one of the primary duties of the Coast Guard will remain keeping smugglers from landing on U.S. shores—just as it was when the Revenue Marine was formed in 1790.

U.S. Coast Guard
DEPARTMENT OF TRANSPORTATION

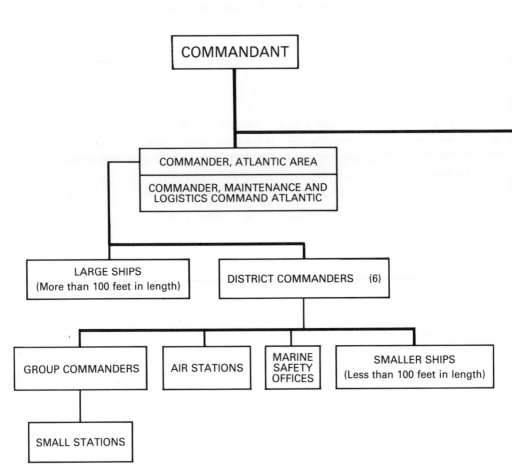

COMMANDANT

COMMANDER, ATLANTIC AREA

COMMANDER, MAINTENANCE AND
LOGISTICS COMMAND ATLANTIC

LARGE SHIPS
(More than 100 feet in length)

DISTRICT COMMANDERS   (6)

GROUP COMMANDERS

AIR STATIONS

MARINE
SAFETY
OFFICES

SMALLER SHIPS
(Less than 100 feet in length)

SMALL STATIONS

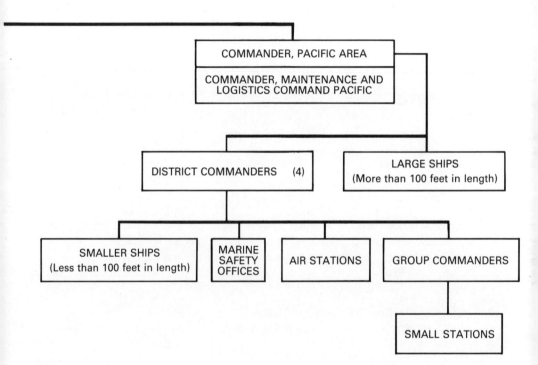

COMMANDER, PACIFIC AREA

COMMANDER, MAINTENANCE AND LOGISTICS COMMAND PACIFIC

DISTRICT COMMANDERS (4)

LARGE SHIPS
(More than 100 feet in length)

SMALLER SHIPS
(Less than 100 feet in length)

MARINE SAFETY OFFICES

AIR STATIONS

GROUP COMMANDERS

SMALL STATIONS

GLOSSARY

Contraband Goods or merchandise of which the importation, exportation, or possession is forbidden.

Cutter A small vessel for use in shallow water, as in loading or unloading cargo ships; also used to refer to all medium-sized and large Coast Guard craft.

Embargo An order of a government that forbids ships to enter or leave its ports.

Ensign The lowest-ranking officer in the Coast Guard.

International Marine Organization A group of more than 100 nations, including the United States, that works to increase international cooperation in matters such as pollution prevention, SAR, and fishing rights.

LORAN-C Long Range Aid to Navigation, a system of electronic transmission from stations around the world that allows mariners to identify their position accurately.

Maritime Having to do with the sea or shipping.

OMEGA A long-range electronic navigational aid that has a greater range and requires fewer stations than LORAN-C.

Poacher One who kills or takes game or fish illegally.

SAR   Search and rescue.

Smuggling   The illegal importation or exportation of goods, especially when tariffs are not paid.

Swab   A Coast Guard recruit or cadet.

Tariff   A tax on imported or exported goods.

SELECTED REFERENCES

Baarslag, Karl. *Coast Guard to the Rescue*. New York: Farrar and Rinehart, 1937.

Bloomfield, Howard Van Lieu. *The Compact History of the United States Coast Guard*. New York: Hawthorn Books, 1966.

Carr, Roland T. *To Sea in Haste*. Washington, DC: Acropolis, 1975.

Donovan, Frank. *The Cutter*. New York: Barnes, 1961.

Engeman, Jack. *The Coast Guard Academy: The Life of a Cadet*. New York: Lothrop, 1957.

Floherty, J. J. *White Terror: Adventures with the Ice Patrol*. Philadelphia: Lippincott, 1947.

Gurney, Gene. *The United States Coast Guard: A Pictorial History*. New York: Crown, 1973.

Johnson, Robert Erwin. *Guardians of the Sea: History of the United States Coast Guard, 1915 to the Present*. Annapolis, MD: Naval Institute Press, 1987.

Kaplan, H. R., and J. F. Hunt. *This Is the Coast Guard*. Cambridge, MD: Cornell Maritime Press, 1972.

Mercer, A.A., ed. *Sea, Surf, and Hell: The U.S. Coast Guard in World War II*. New York: Prentice-Hall, 1945.

O'Brien, T. Michael. *Guardians of the Eighth Sea: A History of the Coast Guard on the Great Lakes*. Columbus, OH: U.S. Government Printing Office, 1976.

Petrow, Richard. *Across the Top of Russia*. New York: McKay, 1967.

Rachlis, Eugene. *The Story of the U.S. Coast Guard*. New York: Random House, 1961.

Stefany, Wallace Charles. *The Department of Transportation*. New York: Chelsea House, 1988.

U.S. Department of Transportation. *Coast Guard History*. Washington, DC: U.S. Department of Transportation and U.S. Coast Guard, 1982.

Villiers, Alan. *Sailing Eagle: The Story of the Coast Guard's Square-Rigger.* New York: Scribners, 1955.

Waters, Harold. *Adventure Unlimited: My Twenty Years of Experience in the Coast Guard.* New York: Prentice-Hall, 1955.

Waters, John M. *Rescue at Sea.* Princeton: Van Nostrand Reinhold, 1966.

Willoughby, Malcom Francis. *Rum War at Sea.* Washington, DC: U.S. Government Printing Office, 1964.

INDEX

Rebecca Stefoff is a Philadelphia-based author and editor who has written more than 25 nonfiction books, many of them for young-adult readers. She holds a Ph.D. in English from the University of Pennsylvania, where she taught from 1974 to 1977. She currently serves as editorial director of the Chelsea House series PLACES AND PEOPLES OF THE WORLD and has contributed the volumes *Arafat* and *King Faisal* to the Chelsea House series WORLD LEADERS.

Arthur M. Schlesinger, jr., served in the White House as special assistant to Presidents Kennedy and Johnson. He is the author of numerous acclaimed works in American history and has twice been awarded the Pulitzer Prize. He taught history at Harvard College for many years and is currently Albert Schweitzer Professor of the Humanities at the City College of New York.